Beautiful MESS

Motherhood for Every Moment

Sherry Surratt & Tracey Eyster

LifeWay Press®
Nashville, Tennessee

ISBN 9781430036494
Item 005692425

Dewey decimal classification: 306.874
Subject headings: MOTHERS \ MOTHERHOOD \ MOTHER-CHILD RELATIONSHIP

Unless otherwise noted, all Scripture quotations are taken from the Holy Bible, NEW INTERNATIONAL VERSION®. Copyright © 1973, 1978, 1984, 2011 by Biblica, Inc. All rights reserved worldwide. Used by permission. Scripture quotations marked (HCSB) are taken from the Holman Christian Standard Bible®, Copyright © 1999, 2000, 2002, 2003, 2009 by Holman Bible Publishers. Used by permission. Holman Christian Standard Bible®, Holman CSB®, and HCSB® are federally registered trademarks of Holman Bible Publishers. Scripture quotations marked (GNT) are from the Good News Translation in Today's English Version— Second Edition Copyright © 1992 by American Bible Society. Used by permission.

To order additional copies of this resource, write to LifeWay Church Resources Customer Service; One LifeWay Plaza; Nashville, TN 37234-0113; fax 615.251.5933; phone 800.458.2772; email *orderentry@lifeway.com;* order online at *www.lifeway.com;* or visit the LifeWay Christian Store serving you.

Printed in the United States of America

Adult Ministry Publishing, LifeWay Church Resources, One LifeWay Plaza, Nashville, TN 37234-0152

CONTENTS

ABOUT THE AUTHORS

SHERRY SURRATT

Sherry (WEEKS 1, 3, AND 5) is the president and CEO of MOPS (Mothers of Preschoolers) International, based in Denver, CO, where she loves encouraging and resourcing moms around the world. Prior to joining MOPS, Sherry served as director of Innovation Labs at Leadership Network and led the children's ministry at Seacoast Church in Mt. Pleasant, SC.

She is the proud mom of two brilliant children, Michael and Brittainy, and beautiful daughter-in-love, Hilary. She's also ridiculously in love with her two beautiful granddaughters, Maggie Claire and Mollie Rose. She resides in Parker, CO, with her husband, Geoff, who serves as a pastor at Southeast Christian and church consultant. Sherry is the co-author of *Just Lead! A No Whining, No Complaining, No Nonsense Practical Guide for Women Leaders in the Church.* Her next book, *Brave Mom: Facing and Overcoming Your Real Mom Fears,* releases in fall 2014.

A special thanks to the MOPS International staff and to my editing partners, Mikkee Hall and Liz Sagaser. Thanks for passionately believing in the power and influence of a mom.

TRACEY LANTER EYSTER

Tracey (WEEKS 2, 4, AND 6) is the happily-in-love wife of Bill and the fun-filled mom of 21-year-old, Samara, and teen son, Westley. She is devoted to her family and is happiest when making memories with them. In 2008, Tracey took her passion for speaking into the lives of moms and created the ministry of *MomLifeToday.com* and thereafter, the live event for moms known as *MomLifeBootCamp.com*. You can find Tracey's voice on Christian radio, as a guest contributor on blogs, in various print magazines, as well as in her first book *Be The Mom*.

Tracey would much rather "be" than "do." On a great day, you will find her taking a hike, writing, or whipping up some home cookin' for family and friends. She lives with her family, and lots of animals, on a horse farm in central Kentucky. An encourager at heart, Tracey enjoys connecting with moms through her personal blog at *BeTheMom.com*, on Facebook *@BeTheMom* and on Twitter *@momblog*.

I'm humbled that God would stir in me a passion for moms that He uses for His purposes and His glory—only He could bring my involvement in this project to fruition. I'm most grateful for Katie Clemens, Linda Treadway, Mitch Temple, and my prayer warriors, who faithfully prayed over the entire *Beautiful Mess* team. Thanks to Evangeline and Marcus Carroll, Kristin and Dan Gaffney, Shannon and Roosevelt Simmons, Kimberly and Steven Sprout, and Mary and John Winkleman. Finally to my husband Bill, daughter, Samara, and son, Westley—thank you for always encouraging me, making memories with me, and making my beautiful mess the greatest joy in my life!

INTRODUCTION

Wherever you are in your parenting journey, being a mother is hard work. It's something none of us fully understood until we were under the pressure of actually raising and guiding another person. Yet motherhood doesn't have to be so overwhelming, and you don't have to feel like everything rests on your shoulders—because God has a plan for you and your children.

Through the next six weeks (or at your own pace) of study, we'll discuss the common struggles of motherhood: *Am I enough? How do I keep from losing myself in this all-consuming role? How can I keep everything in balance?* and *What does God have to say to me about raising kids?* We'll share some of our own parenting fails, lessons we learned along the way, and even precious memories we made.

Six weeks of home study allows you time to consider personal applications and to immerse yourself in Scripture. Journaling—whether in this book or separately—can help you see how God is at work in your life as a mom. Make notes in this book so that you may look back to see how your faith and family are changing for the better.

Each week is broken into five days of reading. Within each day, you'll find Take Action and Dig Deeper sections. We've designed this study with levels of involvement and commitment. Read the days at your own pace. Then, as you're able, apply each day's lesson using Take Action. And if you want or need more depth, work through the Dig Deeper section, too.

We hope this Bible study will encourage you to keep your focus on God as you navigate the joys and pitfalls of motherhood. We want you to feel empowered with the knowledge that God designed you specifically for your children. With His guidance and grace, you can well prepare your children for the future God has planned for them—and maintain your sanity along the way.

ABOUT THE GROUP STUDY

This study is developed around six group sessions. You can complete the study on your own or with other women in a home, office setting, coffee shop, or in a church classroom. Invite a friend or neighbor to join you as your gain insights that will help in your role as a mother.

Ideally, your group will meet for 60-90 minutes each week (or every other week). A church leader, a mom, or a group member can facilitate a group using the suggestions below. Customize them for the needs of your group.

- Pray about your role and participation in this study. Make a commitment to see what God has in store for you. Pray for the other participants and for where God will take all of you during this six-week journey together.

- Arrange for childcare if needed.

- Promote the study through your church. Make sure information is on the church's website, social media sites, and newsletter. Include details about location, times, and childcare, plus who to call for further information. Go to *www.lifeway.com/beautifulmess* to find additional helps.

- Gather basic supplies for each session: name tags, markers, pens, enough books for each group member, and extra Bibles.

- Enlist a volunteer to provide healthy snacks if desired.

- Plan to use name tags for the first two meetings; don't assume everyone knows each other.

- Start each session promptly and honor everyone's time.

GROUP TIME: AM I ENOUGH?

BEAUTIFUL MESS MOMENT

My daughters were 3 and 5 years old at the time, and we had a very busy Saturday planned. They wanted to take a trip. They wanted a pool. And my answer was no, I had things to do at home, and they could be happy playing at home. I don't really recall what I was doing that day, but most likely my head was in a closet, a cabinet, or the dryer. Then it happened—silence. As a mom, you know something is wrong—really wrong— when it gets quiet.

I called for the girls. No answer. I looked in all the rooms and all the hiding places. Nothing. On the brink of panic, I looked in the backyard and then the front. *Surely I would have heard them if they went outside, wouldn't I?* Then my crazy mom mind went to, *Who came in and took them?!*

As I walked into the front yard, I could see them walking down the street. They were only about four houses away, but the fear was overwhelming to think they would go that far that fast … and without me. The girls were fully dressed in boas, sparkly dresses, hats, and plastic bejeweled shoes. Both carried oversized bags and were dragging suitcases on wheels. They were chatting away like it was a normal day.

Holding in my frustration and fear, I started walking their way and called to them, "Where are you going?" The 5-year-old quickly responded, "To a hotel with a pool. Mommy, we told you we wanted to go on a trip and go swimming." When we were finally back in the house and my fear subsided, my first thoughts were: *How did that just happen? Your kids leave the house and you don't even hear them!* And then the thoughts shifted: *How will I ever take care of these girls and protect them in the long run? Can I really do this job? Can I really be the mom they need? Am I enough?*

DISCUSS

Introduce yourself to your group by sharing your name and a beautiful mess moment when you were afraid for your kids or wondered if you were enough as a mom.

☐ *What parts of being a mom are overwhelming or scary for you?*

☐ *Have you been honest with others about your feelings about yourself and what you can't handle on your own? What holds you back from sharing the most embarrassing blunders of motherhood?*

☐ *Many moms feel the need to appear like they are the "perfect mom." Why do you think we put that pressure on ourselves?*

☐ *Read Psalm 23. What are the darkest valleys for moms? What are our greatest fears and insecurities?*

Psalm 23 basically says God has you covered even when you walk through the valley as a mom and you don't know what is coming. He is all you need. He is ready to refresh your weary mom heart. God says we are to bring Him our worries. He knows what moms face and He has enough blessings for this day and the next. We need not fear.

☐ *How are you encouraged by Psalm 23? What word or phrase resonates with you most at this point in life?*

God has you covered. He wants you to look to Him for your strategy for being a mom. And He is there to help you stand firm in the midst of the challenges of motherhood.

☐ *Who are some other people He has placed in your life whom you might lean on for support and help when facing the valleys of motherhood?*

☐ *What are some ways you might build a support system (if you don't have one already) or let supporters know that you appreciate them?*

Take time to dive deeper into the question "Am I enough?" this week. Let God speak to the feelings that are overwhelming and frightening. He is bigger than anything you may face. And He wants to remind you that you are enough in the beautiful mess of motherhood.

WEEK 1

AM I ENOUGH?

Sometimes being a mom can make you feel a bit in over your head. I once heard a comedian quip, "Do you know what it's like to add a third child? It's like being in the swimming pool, holding your two children, and someone throws you another." Exactly. One day you have enough arms, enough patience, enough money, and enough laundry detergent, and then you have children.

Children are an incredible gift from God. Their sweet-smelling baby heads and squishy, chubby thighs can melt your heart in a skinny minute. They can also make you want to run screaming from the room, wondering when was the exact moment that you lost all sense of control. All of a sudden there are a million things to worry about. *Will I know what to do when my baby's fever spikes in the middle of the night? What's the best method to use for potty training? What if they can't make friends in school? How will we ever have enough money for college?* Having children can cause you to question everything about yourself, from your competence to your intelligence and everything in between.

As you dive into this week, I hope there will be moments when you'll say, "Me too." Every mom faces moments when she seriously questions herself. You are not alone with worry, fear, and that nagging question, *Am I enough to handle this?* But I've got great news: God understands this question, and He has some great answers. Together we'll look at the story of King Jehoshaphat, who knew what it felt like to not know his next move, feeling woefully inadequate for the task. His kingdom was to be attacked by several armies, and when he received the report, he quickly realized this situation was bigger than he was. His cry to God—"We do not know what to do, but our eyes are on you"—has the work of moms written all over it. Let's dive in.

DAY 1
THIS FEELS OVERWHELMING.

Michael was my (Sherry's) first adventure into mommyhood. As he lay sleeping soundly in my arms, I remember sitting in the dark quiet of the hospital room, listening to the soft sound of his baby breath. He was perfect. He was mine. And now it was time to take him home.

The thought flicked through my brain, *I wonder if they know I don't know what I'm doing?* ("They" being the nurses who zipped in and out of my room with confident efficiency.) I watched amazed as they swaddled him securely in his little blankets like a little baby burrito with a sweet face. I laid him gently on my bed and tried to copy their movements. We ended up with a baby wad, the blankets knotted up, and Mike's little arms flailing. The list of what I didn't know that I should know was piling up fast.

Then I heard a sound that we would hear again and again over the next few weeks. The sound was part gasp, part gulp and was coming from my tiny son. The noise sounded like a baby bird frantically gasping for his last breath. *What did it mean? Was he choking on something?* My husband's eyes met mine and we shared a silent thought: *What in the world are we supposed to do?*

We rang for the nurse, who reassured us Mike was fine. Being a newborn, his lungs were still immature. While lying down, he might swallow and take in a breath at the same time, causing him to have a gasping reaction. "Perfectly normal" were the words the nurse used. She smiled at me as she said, "He's fine. You'll get used to all the little noises."

I swallowed down the first rumblings of doubt as I was loaded in the wheelchair. *Oh my, they are actually going to let me take this baby home!* Holding my tiny, perfect son in my arms, I pasted a smile on my face, but I could feel my lips trembling. *Surely they will stop me before I make it out the door. They'll figure out I'm a know-nothing mommy who first thought the nasal syringe was something you squeeze to cool the baby off with blasts of air, like a fireplace damper. Any minute now they will discover I'm a mommy impostor who pretends not to gag when changing a poopy diaper, who wants to run the other way screaming at the sight of spit-up.*

I looked around as we came out of the elevator, expecting the baby police to stop me cold: "Ma'am, hand over the baby. You don't know what you're doing!"

And so it began.

I asked myself the questions that I would repeat in my tired mommy brain many times throughout the years to come. *Will I be a good enough mom? Do I have what it takes?*

If you've ever wondered this, you are not alone. Perhaps having a child has caused you to question more than your parenting skills. *Am I smart enough? Do I have the emotional strength and wisdom to raise a healthy, productive adult? Can I provide enough money, enough time, enough of everything my child will need for what life will require?*

Of course you won't, and that's a scary thought.

What are your expectations about being a mom? How have those expectations changed as your child has gotten older?

When you see your child struggling or making bad decisions, how does it make you feel as a mom? Where do you think these feelings come from?

My son is now 27 and the father of two little girls of his own. There were moments when we didn't have the answers, the money, or the wisdom we thought we needed. Over the years my heart has resonated with the words of Jehoshaphat, King of Judah, as he cried out to God for help, knowing there were enemy armies ready to overtake them. He felt inadequate and overwhelmed, and he was honest about it. Take comfort in his words:

For we have no power to face this vast army that is attacking us. We do not know what to do, but our eyes are on you.
2 CHRONICLES 20:12

Have you had a mommy moment when you felt like Jehoshaphat, inadequate and overwhelmed? What were the circumstances that made you feel this way?

Were you surprised by your feelings or did you take them in stride? How did you respond to them?

I can so relate! Many times as parents to Mike and Brittainy, Geoff and I didn't know what our next move was, and we felt out of control. At different times our kids faced discouragement, looking to us for answers and direction. Some of the situations were easy. *Which math class should I take? How will I learn multiplication?*

But other times their situations were far more complex, with scary friendship choices and silences that shut us out. So we prayed. We called on friends and family to pray with us, and we leaned on other parent friends who were a little further down the road. There were times when we didn't feel like we had the strength to pray, so we asked them to pray for us. Though we still faced moments of uncertainty, we felt God's presence just when we needed it. We turned our eyes to a God who was and is bigger than we are.

How about you? Are there areas of your life where you worry you're not enough? Do you sometimes wonder if God knew what He was doing when He made you a mom and gave you the children you have? Mom, you do not have to have all the answers. In fact, you won't always have the answers.

> *What mom fear, large or small, have you not given over to God?*
> *Do you ever worry that maybe even He can't handle it?*

God understands these fears. And yes, God knew exactly what He was doing when He proclaimed you a mom. But there will be moments when you'll realize you can't do it all by yourself.

> *What's your first reaction when you face a situation where you don't know what to do?*

> *As a mom, would you describe yourself as a sharer (you openly share your mom fears with others) or a stuffer (you keep your fears to yourself)? How does this resonate with your personality and how you were raised?*

TAKE ACTION

Do you know how completely loved you are—even on the days everything is a mess? I often struggle with this. I know it in my head, but feeling it in my heart is another issue. I've come to realize that my self-worth is never going to come from how well I do things, like keeping the house spotless or having perfectly-behaved kids. Our craving for approval can be devastating to our souls, making us feel like we're not enough for today or tomorrow. And all the while, God calls us gently to come and know how truly cherished we are. Not because we're enough, Mom, but simply because we're God's beloved daughters.

How can you focus yourself on what you are, instead of what you've failed to do?

DIG DEEPER

Take a moment to read and process the following psalm as it relates to your life.

The LORD is my shepherd, I lack nothing.
He makes me lie down in green pastures,
he leads me beside quiet waters, he refreshes my soul.
He guides me along the right paths for his name's sake.
Even though I walk through the darkest valley,
I will fear no evil, for you are with me;
your rod and your staff, they comfort me.
You prepare a table before me in the presence of my enemies.
You anoint my head with oil; my cup overflows.
Surely your goodness and love will follow me all the days of my life,
and I will dwell in the house of the LORD forever.
PSALM 23

What's God saying to you from this passage?

Moving forward, how can you apply that to your life?

WHERE DO MY INSECURITIES COME FROM?

The day before we took Mike home from the hospital, I remember the pediatric nurses commenting on his soft cry: "Oh you've got a sweet one there. He hardly cries at all." As newborns do, he slept soundly and I had to work hard to rouse him sufficiently so he would nurse. I listened carefully as the nurses talked to me about the importance of making sure I woke him every few hours so he could get the nutrition he needed. Two days after we brought him home from the hospital, I noticed a strange lump on the side of his head. It was soft and squishy and seemed to rise up out of nowhere. I immediately called the pediatrician, who calmly said to bring him in.

As he examined Mike, the doctor began to ask some questions. "Had Mike bumped his head? Had we dropped him or had he fallen off the changing table? Had he been this lethargic since we had brought him home?" I was horrified. The doctor was asking me if Mike had been abused. *He thinks I'm a horrible parent.*

It was a long night. The doctor was also concerned about Mike's yellowish skin color and told us to take him straight to the hospital for a blood test and a scan of his head. As I walked miserably down the hospital corridor, I remember feeling panicky and helpless. *What was the cause of the bump on his head? What did the doctor mean when he said he didn't like the hue of Mike's skin?* Mike looked so tiny and was so dependent on us. As a brand-new mom, I didn't have a clue what to do.

As the test results came back, it was determined that the bump on Mike's head was a normal hematoma from the trauma of birth that went away quickly on its own. The doctor explained that usually these bumps showed up within the initial hours after birth, and while it was unusual that it had taken so long to arise, it was nothing to worry about. The deepened color of his skin was another matter, however. Mike was jaundiced and needed to be put under a light in an incubator to lower his bilirubin. He'd have to stay in the hospital for another couple of days. The doctor remarked that the hematoma, while momentarily concerning, was a blessing. We hadn't noticed Mike's deepened color and, had we not brought him in that evening, the jaundice could have turned into a much more serious matter.

I remember sitting next to my brand-new baby, so incredibly small in the incubator, wearing just his diaper and the eye patches to protect him from the warming light.

As I looked around at all the machinery helping my son's blood levels get back to normal, I was overwhelmed. I felt powerless to do anything but sit beside him. Geoff and I were at the complete mercy of the doctors and nurses to do the right thing. I felt so out of control.

Have you ever felt this way as a mom? You may be feeling like this at this very moment. Maybe your child is facing medical conditions that you can't fix and that won't go away on their own. Or maybe your daughter or son is struggling at school, and you feel powerless to help. Maybe at night you sit waiting for your child to come home, but the clock keeps ticking the minutes by as you sit and wait. As a mom, there are many moments that really are out of our control. It can cause us insecurity, anxiety, and even depression.

What situations as a mom are causing you to feel insecure or out of control?

Jehoshaphat knew what it felt like to have no control. When he received the report of the coming attack, I'm sure he had questions. *How many men? How would the armies attack? When would they arrive and from what direction?* But I'm sure the big question that Jehoshaphat wondered was *How will we stop them?* As he listened to the report, it became evident that he couldn't stop them. They were already on their way. The informants told him that the armies were already closing in.

Let's take a look at how Jehoshaphat responded.

> Alarmed, Jehoshaphat resolved to inquire of the LORD, and he proclaimed a fast for all Judah. The people of Judah came together to seek help from the LORD; indeed, they came from every town in Judah to seek him. Then Jehoshaphat stood up in the assembly of Judah and Jerusalem at the temple of the LORD in the front of the new courtyard and said: "LORD, the God of our ancestors, are you not the God who is in heaven? You rule over all the kingdoms of the nations. Power and might are in your hand, and no one can withstand you."
> 2 CHRONICLES 20:3-6

Here's the incredible comfort I take from this passage: It's OK to feel afraid and know that by yourself you can't handle what might be coming. Hopefully, your insecurities cause you to lean further into God for His strength and wisdom.

This passage used the word "alarmed." As a mom, have you ever felt down-right panicky? Have you ever wondered, *Good grief, now what should I do? I don't have a clue!* For those of us who feel like we need to control everything, this is misery! We want answers, we want solutions, and we want them now! Jehoshaphat probably felt incredible pressure to provide the answers to a kingdom that was surely looking to him for direction. After all, he was the king!

> *As a mom, how do you handle the pressure of knowing the people in your house are depending on you 24/7?*

As your kids get older, their needs change from diapers and nose-wiping to more serious issues with friends, choices, and attitudes. They will bring their broken hearts and bruised emotions to you, and you will want so badly to provide that instant solution and quick fix. But sometimes there isn't one.

Jehoshaphat realized this as well. The armies were coming. He knew they couldn't defend themselves on their own, and running away wasn't going to help. But instead of pretending to have it all under control or becoming paralyzed, he got real. In front of everyone, Jehoshaphat admitted the answers weren't going to come from him, but from the God who rules over all the nations. Jehoshaphat knew he wasn't in control, so he went to the One who was.

TAKE ACTION

It sometimes feels impossible to turn the ultimate control of my life, my marriage, and my children over to a God who sometimes seems so far away. I want the situation solved today, on my terms and my timing. I don't want to wait. Waiting is infuriating, and I want to control all the details—the when, the what, the where—right now.

I can't help but think that God understands my need for control. He reminds me again and again in verses like this one:

> So do not fear, for I am with you;
> do not be dismayed, for I am your God.
> I will strengthen you and help you; I will uphold
> you with my righteous right hand.
> **ISAIAH 41:10**

As a mom, what do you think the words "for I am with you" mean? How can that knowledge change your attitude as a mom?

How does it make you feel when you read that God knows you will be afraid and dismayed? What encouragement does that provide?

God knows we will sometimes be insecure or afraid of what comes at us, and He also knows we will be dismayed at our own inability to handle it. Instead of shaming or condemning, God reminds us that He will strengthen and hold us.

How do you see a need to control playing out in your life as a mom? What can you trust God with today?

DIG DEEPER

Jehoshaphat got ready for battle by calling out to God, assembling the people, and stating God's power out loud. We can call on God in the same way by arming ourselves with some great go-to verses. Here are some of my favorites that remind me of God's power and the fact that He truly is in control.

Look up each verse below. Then write a few sentences of what each means to you. Consider keeping them written in a spot where you'll see them regularly for just the moments you need them.
Isaiah 41:10

Isaiah 58:9a

Proverbs 3:5-6

DAY 3
WHAT'S MY STRATEGY?

Can you recall a moment when being a mom was more messy than beautiful? I remember a story a friend told me of when her twin boys were 3, and she had had one of "those days." All morning long the twins had bickered and fought. They had spread their snack of crackers and jelly all over the carpet, enhanced the living room wallpaper with crayon swirls, and decided the dog would look more handsome with jelly smeared all over his white fur. She tried reasoning and consequences. Everything she tried seemed to do nothing but escalate the behavior.

Exhausted, she sent the boys to their room for some contained playtime, firmly closing the door behind her. At the sound of banging on the wall, she returned to their room to find they had stacked their plastic chairs on top of their toy box and were using their plastic toolset to try to take the door off of its hinges. She said the amazing thing was that they were making progress and had already removed a hinge!

She called me from the garage to relay the story, where she had taken refuge with a bag of Oreos for a much-needed mommy time-out. When I answered the phone, I heard the whispered words, "It's only 10:00 in the morning and I'm already done."

Can your mom heart resonate? Have you had those days when you've tried everything and nothing seems to work—when the frustration keeps coming and coming, and it seems there's no end in sight? Reaching the point where you come to the end of yourself, standing in the garage, barefoot, and clutching a bag of Oreos as you call a friend isn't always such a bad thing. Our weaknesses and struggles nudge us to reach out to others and ultimately show us how much we need God in every detail of our lives.

> *Who is the support system you call when you face overwhelming circumstances or just need encouragement? What are the things they do that support you best?*

King Jehoshaphat knew what it felt like to come to the end of his own might and wisdom. We know the story begins with an intelligence report informing him that numerous armies were on their way to attack them. Verse 3 says that Jehoshaphat was alarmed. He instinctively knew that he couldn't handle what was coming. But instead of becoming paralyzed, he sprang into action. Continuing in 2 Chronicles, we can see Jehoshaphat's strategy and direction.

Take a moment to read 2 Chronicles 20:1-12.

I love the way Jehoshaphat gathered a team of support and help. He called upon his whole kingdom to join him in fasting and prayer, which gave room for God to send special encouragement. Moving forward, Jehoshaphat gets supporting words from a buddy.

> All the men of Judah, with their wives and children
> and little ones, stood there before the LORD.
> Then the Spirit of the LORD came on Jahaziel son of Zechariah,
> the son of Benaiah, the son of Jeiel, the son of Mattaniah, a
> Levite and descendant of Asaph, as he stood in the assembly.
> He said: "Listen, King Jehoshaphat and all who live in
> Judah and Jerusalem! This is what the LORD says to you:
> 'Do not be afraid or discouraged because of this vast
> army. For the battle is not yours, but God's.'"
> 2 CHRONICLES 20:13-15

Mom, you're not alone, and God has your back. Even when we don't think or feel like we have a strategy to do this motherhood thing, God does. But many times it takes our acknowledgment that we need help for these words to come. Investing effort into forming a support team of those who will encourage you in the most desperate moments is so worth it!

> *What is, or could be, your go-to strategy for when being a mom seems overwhelming or scary?*

I remind myself again and again of the way that Jehoshaphat got his eyes off himself and put them on God. He did this through a gigantic worship service.

> Jehoshaphat bowed down with his face to the ground, and all
> the people of Judah and Jerusalem fell down in worship before
> the LORD. ... After consulting the people, Jehoshaphat appointed
> men to sing to the LORD and to praise him for the splendor of
> his holiness as they went out at the head of the army, saying:
> "Give thanks to the LORD, for his love endures forever."
> 2 CHRONICLES 20:18,21

In other words, Jehoshaphat had a gigantic worship party, loud and strong! It sounds like there was singing, dancing, and shouting. They didn't hold back. There's nothing like bold and courageous worship to remind us of our total dependence on God, and this is exactly what Jehoshaphat did. He proclaimed, "We can't do this on our own, God. We are counting on You! Bring it on!"

The passage ends with a surprising triumph for Jehoshaphat. Not only were they victorious, but God arranged it so they didn't even have to fight. The enemy armies had turned on each other.

> When the men of Judah came to the place that overlooks
> the desert and looked toward the vast army, they saw only
> dead bodies lying on the ground; no one had escaped.
> **2 CHRONICLES 20:24**

Isn't it just like God to take care of the situation in ways they couldn't even have dreamed of?

Jehoshaphat was wise to not freeze or throw up his hands when faced with attacking armies. He formed a strategy of declaring, sharing, and worshiping. He shouted out loud that he knew they couldn't do this on their own but that he knew the God who could. He shared his fear and invited others to join him in beseeching God. He called everyone to come and worship.

As you consider the actions of Jehoshaphat, think about how it could apply to your life. Jehoshaphat declared God's power, he shared the situation and need with his kingdom, and then he led the people in worship.

What does worship mean to you?

How does your heart resonate with God in worship? The Bible says that when we worship God, we draw close to Him and He not only hears us, but He responds. James 4 tells us to "draw near to God, and he will draw near to you" (v. 8, ESV). Worship connects us to God in a way nothing else does. Worship can happen anywhere at any time, opening the door for God to speak intimately to our hearts.

Consider some ways your heart connects to God. Is it memorizing Scripture and thanking Him for the guidance of His Word? Is it being outdoors and enjoying the beauty of nature, acknowledging that God is the Author of it? Is it watching your children and appreciating how wonderful and beautiful God made them? Is it listening to a worship song or even singing it out to God in praise? Take some time to think about how your heart responds best to God and spend some concentrated time this week devoted to those things.

TAKE ACTION

One of the first steps in Jehoshaphat's strategy was to call on others to cry out to God with him. It can be an incredible gift when another mom puts her arms around you and says, "It's going to be all right." She can join you in prayer for the things you're facing. Imagine having an entire group of moms you can lean into for encouragement and prayer. Consider these possibilities:

• If you're a mom of preschoolers, think about joining a MOPS group or starting a gathering of moms at your church. This is a friendship circle of moms who gather regularly to grow together as moms, wives, leaders, and friends. Go to *www.mops.org* and *www.momlifetoday.com* for more information.

• Join a small group at your church. If your church doesn't have any available, consider starting a moms group of your own. There are numerous Bible studies at *www.lifeway.com/women* that you could work through together.

DIG DEEPER

We can easily get so distracted with our never-ending to-do list that we forget to stop and take in the moment. We become so overwhelmed at the thought of tomorrow that we forget to focus on today. Take time to breathe in your kids. Notice their little hands and toes. Pay attention to their sweet smiles and desire to spend time with you. Enjoy the gift you have today.

Yet, go one further. The second step in Jehoshaphat's strategy was worship. Take time right now to thank the One who gave you your children. Spend some energy worshiping Him for His goodness, mercy, love, and provision for you and your kids. Do you have a regular rhythm of worshiping God that connects you directly to His power and spirit? Worshiping God can include singing, but it can also include journaling, reciting verses aloud, enjoying the beauty of nature, and others ways that your heart can resonate with His. Consider trying a new rhythm of worship this week, and then share it with a friend.

DAY 4
I WILL STAND FIRM.

Several years ago, I led a collaborative leadership cohort of women who led at high levels in their churches. One of the women shared a story of a difficulty she was having with another woman in her church. She kept hearing from others that this woman was talking behind her back and spreading stories about her. She said it was incredibly discouraging. She had tried on numerous occasions to sit down with the woman to work through the situation, but nothing seemed to help. She had apologized for whatever had caused the hard feelings, had tried to befriend the woman, and had covered their relationship with prayer, but still it continued. She said it was a wakeup call when her husband said, "Have you ever considered that there may be more going on here than just that this woman is upset with you? Maybe Satan is trying to discourage you."

This leader shared the story with us to enlist our help. She said she felt like she needed a wide circle of prayer support, a team of women who would commit to praying for her on a regular basis, especially during the moments when discouragement hit. She called us her S.W.A.T. team, copying the Army acronym for "Special Weapons and Tactics." She asked us to use all of the weapons of spiritual warfare that we knew—praying for her, declaring Scriptures over her, speaking godly encouragements on her behalf, and so forth. I felt honored to be a part of this team. Though we didn't live near each other, this leader would occasionally send out an email to us all that simply said, "Today, I'm facing some discouragement. Would you stand with me?" And we would. It was incredible to be a part of the email chain as these women, who knew what it was like to face discouragement, all piled in with their prayers and encouragements. We would respond with verses, a written prayer, or other form of encouragement. Sometimes one of us would just pick up the phone and call to lift her spirits.

> *Satan often comes after us in an area in which he knows we're easily discouraged. Have you noticed a particular pattern that Satan uses?*

Moms, if you're facing a deep sense of doubt in being a mom—if you feel fear and a deep sense of inadequacy on a regular basis—could there be more going on than simple insecurity? Here's one thing I know: Satan doesn't want you to succeed as a mom. He wants you to feel like you can't, like you aren't enough, like you're failing. He is the Enemy of our soul, and he wants the exact opposite of what God wants for you.

> Be alert and of sober mind. Your enemy the devil prowls
> around like a roaring lion looking for someone to devour.
> **1 PETER 5:8**

God wants you to know you are the exact right mom for your children—that through Him you are enough. He will equip you with everything you need as you call daily on Him. Satan knows that when you connect with the God of the nations, you are a powerful force. As a mom, you're raising the generation of tomorrow, and Satan wants to stop you any way he can. Could some of your discouragement be coming from Satan?

Have you sensed deep times of discouragement as a mom? What do
you do to combat them?

I have good news. You don't have to stand for it. When you're a daughter of the King, Satan has no power over you. Jehoshaphat's friend Jahaziel reminded him of this too:

> He said: "Listen, King Jehoshaphat and all who live in
> Judah and Jerusalem! This is what the LORD says to you:
> 'Do not be afraid or discouraged because of this vast
> army. For the battle is not yours, but God's.'"
> **2 CHRONICLES 20:15**

Moms, the battle of discouragement that Satan will try to engage us in is not ours alone. God proved long ago that He is more powerful than anything Satan might try to throw at us. Satan wants us to get mired in our piles of laundry and the fact that our kids can't keep their rooms clean or keep up with their homework. He wants us to feel overwhelmed at every rebellious choice our kids make and every time they shut down into a silent wall of resentment. We might hear Satan's whisper in our ear, "You are not enough of a mom to handle this." That's when we must remind ourselves Whose battle it really is and Who has already won it.

> You will not have to fight this battle. Take up your positions;
> stand firm and see the deliverance the LORD will give you, Judah
> and Jerusalem. Do not be afraid; do not be discouraged. Go
> out to face them tomorrow, and the LORD will be with you.
> **2 CHRONICLES 20:17**

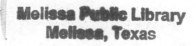

Jahaziel was reminding Jehoshaphat and the people of Judah that they needn't even worry how God would take care of it. It was His problem, His battle, and all the people had to do was stand firm.

As you consider this passage and Jahaziel's encouragement to Jehoshaphat, think about the applications it could have in your mom life.

Do you have a Jahaziel in your life who speaks truth into you when you need to stand firm? If you do, remember to tell her how important she is in your life. If you don't, start by seeking a prayer partner or mom mentor.

Who else can you call to help you stand firm in your role as a mother? What are the ways they can best help you?

Jahaziel told Jehoshaphat that they would not have to fight the battle but to take up their positions. In what ways can we, as moms, take up our positions?

Every mom needs a friend who understands her and will stand beside her during those discouraging moments. On your S.W.A.T. team, your friends can serve various roles. Do you have a friend you can pray with? How about a special mom friend who is your encourager? Do you have a wise mom friend who can share sage advice? How about a mom friend to recite encouraging Scripture to you? If you don't, start small! Start by choosing one mom friend to do just one of these things.

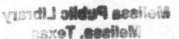

TAKE ACTION

When you feel overwhelmed and as though you're being attacked by Satan, remember that Scripture reassures us that God fights for us—and He will win. Beside each verse, list how it can encourage you in the midst of the battle. Post the one that speaks most to you where you will see it often.

A thief comes only to steal and to kill and to destroy. I have come so that they may have life and have it in abundance.
JOHN 10:10 (HCSB)

The God of peace will soon crush Satan under your feet. The grace of our Lord Jesus be with you.
ROMANS 16:20

Do not give the devil a foothold.
EPHESIANS 4:27

Submit yourselves, then, to God. Resist the devil, and he will flee from you.
JAMES 4:7

This is the confidence we have in approaching God: that if we ask anything according to his will, he hears us. And if we know that he hears us—whatever we ask—we know that we have what we asked of him. ... We know that we are children of God, and that the whole world is under the control of the evil one. We know also that the Son of God has come and has given us understanding, so that we may know him who is true. And we are in him who is true by being in his Son Jesus Christ. He is the true God and eternal life.
1 JOHN 5:14-15,19-20

DIG DEEPER

Ephesians 6 talks about spiritual warfare and putting on the armor of God. Read the entire chapter and make a list of the ways you'll enlist the armor of God in your warfare against discouragement as a mom.

GOD IS BIGGER THAN ANY SITUATION I WILL FACE.

When our daughter, Brittainy, was in middle school, I began to notice that she was becoming increasingly withdrawn. One night while we were at a movie together, she got up and went to the restroom. When she didn't come right back, I went to search for her and was surprised to find her lying on a bench in the lobby, surrounded by the theater staff. Pale and sweaty, she looked up at me and said words that made my blood run cold: "Mom, I think I'm having a heart attack." What? She was 13 years old. How could a young, healthy 13-year-old be having a heart attack? I tried to swallow down a feeling of panic as we rushed her to a nearby emergency room. It wasn't long before the doctor pulled me aside and shared what he thought was going on. He assured me Brittainy's heart was fine, but she was experiencing palpitations, tightness in her chest, and an overwhelming sense of fear. Brittainy was having a panic attack.

I didn't know anything about panic attacks. I thought they were just feelings of nervousness. Over the next few months as my daughter experienced more of these, sometimes more than one a day, I learned that they are debilitating. They make you want to run, but you don't know what you are running from. They are not just feelings of panic, but overwhelming experiences that come out of nowhere, taking you completely by surprise.

As a mom, I wanted to do anything I could to help my beautiful, athletic daughter from experiencing these horrible things. I wanted them to stop—and to stop this instant. We talked with the doctor. We explored medication. We prayed together. We tried to figure out where they were coming from and why they first started. There weren't many answers that brought my mom heart the peace it was looking for.

I noticed my prayer life began to change. My times with God took on a new desperation. *Please God. Please take these away. Please God. I don't understand. Please God, do something.* I felt desperate because it seemed like God wasn't doing anything at all. When I prayed, I got no answer. I watched my daughter struggle week after week.

Jehoshaphat's answer came immediately. He got the report, he prayed, he praised, and he stood firm. The battle was swift and triumphant. Jehoshaphat and his army stood on the hill and looked over all the dead bodies. God was right.

As they began to sing and praise, the LORD set ambushes against the men of Ammon and Moab and Mount Seir who were invading Judah, and they were defeated. The Ammonites and Moabites rose up against the men from Mount Seir to destroy and annihilate them. After they finished slaughtering the men from Seir, they helped to destroy one another.
2 CHRONICLES 20:22-23

Boom. Done. At times I read that story and wonder why God sometimes moves instantly and other times it seems to take years. Why? And when God does take longer to answer, why doesn't He explain it?

Is there something concerning your family that you've been praying about for a long time? As you read verses about God's faithfulness and love for you, what doubts do you have?

One day several months later Brittainy asked me if I would take a cake decorating class with her. The class was expensive, we'd have to get up early on Saturdays, and we'd have to buy a big list of supplies. No, I really didn't want to spend my Saturdays decorating cakes. This wasn't my thing. But the look in my daughter's eyes was wistful: "Mom, let's do something fun."

We did take that class, and we were the worst two students in the room. My icing roses were lopsided. I never did master how to properly create a petal leaf. More icing went in my mouth than on the cakes. When the instructor would observe the other students, she would exclaim, "Excellent technique!" When she would pass Brittainy and I, she would smile and say, "How about if we keep trying?" While we will never be featured on a cooking show, I am so glad we took that class. Over the course of the weeks, I saw God's hand. Brittainy teased me about my sad attempts at buttercream frosting. We laughed and enjoyed each other. We were able to talk about silly things, which led to more important things—like God's faithfulness, His love for us, and His healing hand that doesn't always work according to our time schedule.

Why might God work quickly in some situations and slowly in others?

Have you seen God move slowly or quickly in your life? What can you learn from this?

One Saturday I sat on the couch, looking back over a journal entry I had written a year earlier. It was full of pain and questions, smack in the middle of the time when Brittainy's panic attacks were at their worst. I felt God whisper to my heart, *You thought I wasn't working, but I was.* Indeed He was. Today, Brittainy is an incredibly compassionate young woman, able to talk to other girls about panic attacks and how they've never completely gone away but how she sees God in them. She tells other girls about God's healing hand and how it moves quickly and slowly. But it always moves.

In my journal, I had written these verses from Ephesians:

> I pray that you, being rooted and established in love, may
> have power, together with all the Lord's holy people, to grasp
> how wide and long and high and deep is the love of Christ,
> and to know this love that surpasses knowledge—that you
> may be filled to the measure of all the fullness of God.
> **EPHESIANS 3:17-19**

Mom, this is my prayer for you, that you will know how great God's love is for you. God's bigger than anything you could ever face with your kids. His love is wide and long and high and deep and covers every insecurity you could ever have. By yourself, you can never be enough, but through Him, you're more than a conqueror. May you be filled up in this.

In what ways do you see God's incredible love working in your life?

Who could you share this news with this week?

TAKE ACTION

When I was going through the difficult period with Brittainy, I started a gratitude journal, listing blessings from God. Sometimes I didn't feel like writing anything at all, but as I continued my list, I felt God work in my heart. Consider starting your own gratitude journal. See how many things you can list. Be sure to invest time in reading back over your lists in the days to come. You might be surprised how much God has moved in your life.

DIG DEEPER

Is your mom heart searching for peace? God's Word can help.

> I remain confident of this:
> I will see the goodness of the LORD
> in the land of the living.
> Wait for the LORD;
> be strong and take heart
> and wait for the LORD.
> **PSALM 27:13-14**

> But he said to me, "My grace is sufficient for you, for my power is made perfect in weakness." Therefore I will boast all the more gladly about my weaknesses, so that Christ's power may rest on me.
> **2 CORINTHIANS 12:9**

> Let the peace of Christ rule in your hearts, since as members of one body you were called to peace. And be thankful. Let the message of Christ dwell among you richly as you teach and admonish one another with all wisdom through psalms, hymns, and songs from the Spirit, singing to God with gratitude in your hearts. And whatever you do, whether in word or deed, do it all in the name of the Lord Jesus, giving thanks to God the Father through him.
> **COLOSSIANS 3:15-17**

Let your heart sink into these passages. Ask God to transform you through it.

What could God be saying to you about His timing and work?

GROUP TIME:
HOW CAN I LOVE THIS MESS?

BEAUTIFUL MESS MOMENT

It was a day when the chauffeur hat went on and didn't come off for several hours. It was summer. It was hot and muggy, and we were spending the majority of the afternoon stuck in the car while running errands. As I listened to my kids chat in the back seat, I thought it was odd that they were discussing different people I knew nothing about: "She was sweet." or "He was cupcake sweet." But hey, everyone was happy, so I just kept driving.

My first clue was when the man in a vehicle next to me gave me a dirty look. Then the laughing erupted, and I heard the phrase, "He is so sour!" I quickly discovered the kids were playing "sweet or sour" in which they wave or blow kisses to the people in other cars. Depending upon their response, the people were labeled sweet or sour. It got me thinking, *That day the kids would label me sweet, but how many days would they label me sour?*

DISCUSS

- *What were some of your sweet or sour moments this week?*

- *Describe a recent time in your home when your bad attitude rubbed off on other family members.*

- *What are the situations or circumstances that get to you the most and bring out the sourness and bad attitudes?*

Some days are like that—they are sour. No matter what you do or how hard you try, things just go sour. And you know what? It's OK that everyday is not perfect. It's alright to have some sour mixed in with the sweet. Without the sour, we never realize how sweet the sweet really is. But even on the sour days, motherhood can be beautiful even when it's a mess. So how can we learn to love the mess?

☐ *Read Psalm 147:3. What has broken your heart? What has wounded you?*

☐ *What truths or promises do you learn from this verse?*

Discouragement, disheartenment, shame, failure, and fear will weigh us down and cause us to experience more sour days.

☐ *How might God heal your broken heart, bind up your wounds, or make a new heart spring up in you?*

☐ *Why do we doubt that God wants to help us?*

☐ *Read James 4:7-8. If you were to separate the truths associated with God and the truths associated with the Devil, what would you find?*

The Devil will do all he can to keep us hiding from God and focused on all the ways we are a mess. God does just the opposite. He desires that we draw near to Him and allow Him to clean up the mess. God wants us to find the beauty and grace in messy.

<u>God</u>	<u>Devil</u>

☐ *How does this clip encourage you? What other positive words would you use to describe your role as a mom?*

This week, as you think about life during your homework, remember that you're being equipped for the good work that is motherhood, raising the next generation with all its sweet and sour moments.

WEEK 2

HOW CAN I LOVE THIS MESS?

It's Mother's Day. She awakens from her slumber, and as she stretches in relaxation, a faint noise causes her to stiffen in silence. Through squinted eyes she concentrates hard, deciphering what her cloudy-from-sleep brain is hearing. With an emotion bordering on sheer panic, she springs from the bed, bolts down the stairs, turns the corner and sees ... terror, right there in her kitchen. Her three young children stand dripping in various sticky substances, surrounded by the inglorious mess that once was her sparkly, germ-free, pristine kitchen. Her oh-so-proud daughter shrieks, "Happy Day of Mothers!"

Happy Mother's Day indeed.

Motherhood is a beautiful gift that you can unwrap daily, revealing new wonders of who your children are becoming and how God can use your gifts and talents in His process of molding them. Unfortunately for moms, our "I want everything to be just perfect in my home" expectations do not always meet and greet even our typical days, much less the ones we hope to be special occasions. Motherhood is messy, but oh how we long for the serene.

DAY 1
WHY WE DOUBT

Imagine, if you will, a home filled with peace and tranquility. A home where everything is neat and tidy, everyone's needs are met with joy, screaming ceases, fighting flutters away, and relationships built on love blossom all around. OK, stop laughing ... or crying ... and stick with me here. You are about to learn something that will resonate so deeply within your soul that it might astound you—at least it did me.

Once this divine knowledge seems less distant in its "epicness," it will make it easy to reach out and grab on those days when you want to reach out and grab one of your kids and growl at them. And it will help you cut yourself some slack when you want to magnify your perceived failures as a mom. (At least that's what I do when messy happens.)

See that dark tunnel of a non-peace-filled home that is your reality? There is a light at the end of the tunnel. If peace sounds like bliss to you—and something you long for in your own home—that's because it's the way each of us was designed by God to live. We intuitively and inherently long for tranquility because that's how we started out. The haven we long for our homes to be is a memory of the future put deep within our souls by the Creator of the universe and revealed to us in His Word. At one point, we had paradise—everything we could want or need.

> So God created mankind in his own image, in the image of God he created them; male and female he created them. God blessed them and said to them, "Be fruitful and increase in number; fill the earth and subdue it. Rule over the fish in the sea and the birds in the sky and over every living creature that moves on the ground." Then God said, "I give you every seed-bearing plant on the face of the whole earth and every tree that has fruit with seed in it. They will be yours for food. And to all the beasts of the earth and all the birds in the sky and all the creatures that move along the ground—everything that has the breath of life in it—I give every green plant for food." And it was so.
> **GENESIS 1:27-30**

Close your eyes and bask in the description when we had it all. Imagine how we were created to live. Bliss and harmony, with what we needed all around us—including God.

Go back and highlight everything in those verses that God did to provide for us.

*Describe what a day in the garden of Eden might look like for you,
if you could be transported there.*

God walked in the garden of Eden with Adam and Eve, and He created for them all they could possibly need. He even dwelled with them there. Doesn't that give you goose bumps?

*What emotions are stirred up in you when you read about the
garden of Eden and how life was supposed to be?*

Describe how you would like things to be in your home.

On my really bad days, I (Tracey) chant in my mind (and sometimes even out loud), "cabin in the woods, cabin in the woods" because that would be my bliss and peaceful setting. My cabin in the woods would have everything I need, just like Adam and Eve's garden of Eden. In fact, if given some lumber and tools, I could actually build a cabin in the woods down to the last detail because I've spent so much time there in my mind.

Now even though my cabin in the woods is me daydreaming about an escape, the way God has used that thought in my mind is that I now know that when I think or say "cabin in the woods," it is actually a trigger for me to realize what is really going on in my head and heart. It is a signal to my longing for the garden of Eden, peace, and actually an indicator that I am craving time with God.

*What recurring thought for escape pops into your mind whenever
you start to feel stressed or overwhelmed?*

We all have that craving. We can fill that craving with things other than God, but that craving—gone unsatisfied by the real nourishment we seek—leads to all the wrong places: purchasing more stuff, eating more food, escaping for more sleep or substances to numb us, or engaging in conversations (especially conversations through social media) to avoid the real Voice we seek.

When you feel overwhelmed, stressed, or long for something but aren't quite sure what it is, where do you attempt to meet that need?

God wants you to know He has a much wiser solution to our longings. My cabin in the woods fantasy is actually my longing for the peace and tranquility of the garden, where I was supposed to walk and talk with God daily. Your _____ (however you answered question above) is your longing for the garden.

> Taste and see that the LORD is good;
> blessed is the one who takes refuge in him.
> PSALM 34:8

Look up the definition for "refuge," or write your own definition. Then list some synonyms of "refuge."

The blessed truth, Mom, is that motherhood is an area in your life God can use to bring you to the end of yourself so that you will seek Him. While it seems counterintuitive, the stresses and strife in your life are a bonus of motherhood. Take a moment to allow that to sink in.

Because sanctuary with Him and strolling with Him in the garden is our heritage, when we find ourselves the most overwhelmed is when we need to take that "I need my cabin in the woods" warning light as a divine clue to go straight to God.

Read Psalm 42:1-2. Answer the question found in verse 2: "When can I come and appear before God?"

We can meet with God anywhere, anytime because Jesus Christ came to earth to give us a way to go directly to God for help. So, Mom, if you need help, if you're overwhelmed, the good news is this: seek God.

It's amazing to realize that we don't have to go to the garden of Eden, the cabin in the woods, the beach, the lake, or anywhere else to meet with God. We have the ability

every day to meet with Him. And the reason we long for time with God is that when we are with Him, He soothes us, He comforts us, and He provides peace.

We know our children cry out to us when they need us, and we respond. How comforting is it to know your Father will do the same for you?

Hopefully we will not wait until we are at fever pitch before we seek Him! (Forgive me, I just had a flashback to the first few months with my colic-plagued son—not pretty, not pretty at all.) Moms, we can have a piece of what heaven will be like right here on earth if we pursue spending time with God. You don't have to go to a "place" to do that. God is where you are. In our hectic day-to-day, carving out time can be hard. But we all can start somewhere.

Jot down a time(s) in your day when you could linger with God.

TAKE ACTION

Filling the longing for the garden and God can be found in the practice of seeking His presence. It is worth the effort, because in a world filled with chaos, the dividends of peace are what your soul longs for. Start by simply sitting in silence for five minutes, constantly redirecting your thoughts back to God when they wander. Just the act of silence in your day is an amazing practice to cultivate. By having your kids quietly play on their own, they will ultimately learn this same life-giving discipline.

DIG DEEPER

For some additional time with God, read Psalm 25. Write down all the ways David seeks to be led by the Lord. Write each of these words separately on sticky notes and put them in various places in your home—inside a cabinet door, above the sink, on the laundry detergent, on your calendar or computer, on the back of your door at work, on your dashboard in the car, on your checkbook, above the diaper-changing table—you get the idea. Throughout the week, when you're feeling overwhelmed or stressed out, before that longing for the garden even tugs at your heart, a quick glance at all God is waiting to do for you will help you make it through your week with more assurance that you are not alone; He indeed is with you.

DAY 2
BELIEVING THE DECEIVER

When I was 5 years old, I was a bit of a picky eater, and I had a very hard time with vegetables. On a lovely summer evening, after dinner was over for everyone but me, I made a decision that has lived in Lanter family infamy. I vividly remember the last words from my dad's mouth as he left the kitchen: "You are not to get up from that table until those vegetables are gone, young lady." Well, at some point the vegetables were gone (not technically eaten), so I got up from the table and left for my friend's house, bursting at the seams to meet the puppies just born at her home.

I was having such fun frolicking in puppy paradise until my brother walked into my neighbor's garage and said, "You have to get home now. You're in big trouble. Dad found the vegetables you didn't eat." That was the longest, scariest walk of my life. I was fearful, ashamed, and sweating buckets because I had lied to my dad, and I knew I was caught red-handed. Yet I was most afraid of facing my father because I knew he was going to be disappointed in me. If my brother hadn't marched me home, I may not have made it back. Shame is powerful, obviously, because I remember so many details of that event from so long ago. Even so, I'm blessed to have grown up in a home filled with love and understanding. We had our own issues, but I always knew I was loved and safe. God's ways were taught and modeled. I've also had a peek into life in other homes where I've seen turmoil and strife—yelling, hitting, name-calling, inappropriate behaviors brought on by too much excess, and abrasive personalities.

The garden of Eden reveals God's care and pursuit of man. Conversely, the garden also exposes a very real and present Enemy who pursues us as well. Eve was deceived by that Enemy, and Mom, if you're not aware, that same Enemy is working overtime today to influence and whisper lies to you. The Enemy knows that "the hand that rocks the cradle rules the world," and he is keen on negatively influencing the head and heart behind that hand—as well as the little ones those hands are guiding.[1]

There is a real Enemy who wants to keep you from knowing how loved you are by God, and that Enemy will whisper lies to you just as he did to Eve in the garden. No matter the home you came from or the issues in your home now, you have the power to beat back the lies of the Enemy. You hold all the power when you walk through life with Father God.

Read how God's Word describes the Enemy versus our Provider in John 10:10.

The Enemy/thief _____

Jesus our Provider _____

Read what happened in the garden when Eve was confronted by the Enemy:

> Now the serpent was more crafty than any of the wild animals
> the LORD God had made. He said to the woman, "Did God
> really say, 'You must not eat from any tree in the garden'?"
> **GENESIS 3:1**

How do you see the Enemy trying to persuade the woman?

God created a family, giving them a wonderful place to live. Then the Enemy of God slithered over to Eve, questioned her, and cast doubt on the Creator of the universe. And Eve started chatting with him. Why, oh why, do we listen?

I went through a period of time when my children were toddlers in which I really started to feel like I was blowing it as a mom. I just felt that I could never quite stay ahead of all that needed to get done, and I also felt that I wasn't living up to expectations. Here's the thing, the expectations were my own. And those expectations were built around my desire to look like I had it all together. Since I couldn't live up to that impossible image, I shut myself out from the world.

Describe a time as a mom when you felt you weren't good enough.

Go back and write in large letters over the top of that sentence "LIE."

I think it is time we all admitted that we don't have it all together—and we are not expected to. What better way does the Enemy have than to defeat us in our own minds and steal our joy?

The right attitude toward motherhood will empower us to live in joy.
Write out Proverbs 17:22.

I frequently hear from moms who had never truly recognized their biggest problem with motherhood is their attitude toward it. They realize they allow lies about themselves to play over and over again in their own minds. Whether suffering from the Enemy's lies or their own mistakes, they keep chastising themselves for it. Frustrations brought on by motherhood lead to a bad attitude that gets worse based on their frustration level. Either way, it is not who they are that's the problem; it's what they have come to believe about themselves or their role as mother.

Evangelist D.L. Moody once said, "Attitudes determine our actions, for good or bad." Mom, you are in a battle for your attitude! What we believe about ourselves and God trickles down to our children. And when we have a bad attitude toward ourselves, our circumstances, or our God, our kids will pick up on it and join us. Finish this sentence for me: "If mama ain't happy, _____"

Mom, don't beat yourself up. You are in a battle. It's time to learn how to better ignore the lies. It may seem over the top to see this as a battle. But let's think about this together. Just who is it who wants you to be unhappy, frustrated, overwhelmed, down-trodden, and in a lousy attitude? The same Enemy who wants you to question your value as a mom and the God-given role you have in your home.

> *Read Proverbs 23:25. Do I hear hissing? Who wants to oppose that truth found in Scripture?*

> Be alert and of sober mind. Your enemy the devil prowls around like a roaring lion looking for someone to devour.
> 1 PETER 5:8

> *What does the word "devour" mean to you?*

Not only does the Enemy want to devour you, he wants to devour your kids. Mom, Eve's mistake of listening to the Enemy does not need to be a mistake that you and I also make. If you realize hissing lies when you hear them, you can stop them dead in their tracks.

> *Read 2 Thessalonians 3:3. What areas in your life are God and Satan vying for authority in the way you speak or think about yourself?*

That longing for the garden will help you to resist the Enemy and draw you to the care of Father God who will always protect and care for you.

My teen son is home as I write this, and he really likes my tuna-fish salad with boiled eggs, so I put some eggs on the stove to cook. Busy writing, I forgot about the eggs—until I heard a loud bang. My son and I ran to the kitchen to discover egg splatters all over my stove. The next words out of my mouth would be very telling. Even as a teenager, my son sees and files away reactions to the everyday. A whisper tugged at my heart, *What a beautiful mess. In a few short months, he'll fly the nest and making tuna-fish salad for him will be a memory. How would I want this memory to settle into his mind?* I started laughing and pointing out the mess. Then I celebrated with him the good news that we still had eggs, so lunch would be a little late.

What I saw as a natural disaster, he thought was cool—quite the science experiment on what happens when a trapped liquid turns to a solid via high heat. In the end, we laughed about it, and hopefully it will serve as a teaching moment. Someday he will be a daddy, and when one of his kids spills a full glass of milk all over the kitchen, I hope he will laugh and share a memory of the time his mom burned the eggs!

Let's learn to see our beautiful messes as a teaching tool for our children.

TAKE ACTION

Write out a promise to yourself, agreeing to see your beautiful messes as opportunities to teach, share, laugh, make a memory, or whatever words you choose that depict truth: even a beautiful mess can be used for God's purposes.

DIG DEEPER

We all have something about us that we work hard to keep hidden from the world. The Enemy knows this, and he delights in magnifying our struggles. The best way to over-power the lies of the Enemy is to saturate your mind with the truth of who God says you are! Read the following verses and write beside each what God says about you. Consider writing the truths you discover on an index card and reading over it every morning before you get out of bed and every evening before you turn out the light.

Genesis 1:27   *John 1:12*
Psalm 139:14   *Ephesians 2:10*

DAY 3
HIDING FROM GOD WHILE ACHING TO BE HEARD

I asked one of my dearest friends to sing on my wedding day, and she had chosen the perfect dress to wear for the occasion. Imagine my surprise when, instead, she showed up on the big day wearing a business suit. It seems her sweet toddler son had decided to help make her dress "prettier" by coloring it with his most favorite green permanent marker. For her, bigger than the problem of a dress more colorful than she had intended was the problem that her son knew what he did was wrong—that whole "willful disobedience" vs. "still learning the rules" struggle. When she located him, he was hiding behind the curtains of her home with his head down, too forlorn to even look up into her eyes.

We all have things in our past and in our daily lives that could leave us hiding behind the curtains and avoiding eye contact with everyone who knows us.

For me, those major "I blew it as a mom" moments used to leave me *knowing* that I had just ruined my kids for life. I have done things I am ashamed of—and literally just broke out in a cold sweat thinking about a couple of them. What's worse, I usually start thinking about my mistakes while lying in bed at night, and then there goes a good night's sleep—which makes me grouchy the next day, which leads to increased snarkyness, paving the way for the "I am a raving lunatic mother, and my kids are ruined for life" cycle that bounces around in my overstressed, overstimulated mommy brain. Instantly, I'm stress-paralyzed. Deep, cleansing breaths.

> *What one mistake (or ten) are you thinking about? Jot them down.*
> *(Or not ... you don't have to go there!)*

Paralyzing stress leads to hiding behind a curtain from God. I mean, really, if I am in my "very worst mom ever" frame of mind, the last place my frustrated, defeated self wants to go is to God. He, no doubt, is totally uninterested in me. He doesn't even want to look upon me. He is *so* done with me.

Have you been there? Drowning in lies?

Oh, sweet Mom, I hope you will hear this loud and clear. Much of what you beat yourself up over has gotten so much bigger in your mind than in anyone else's that you're wasting precious energy. We moms truly seem to be our own worst enemies—or perhaps our worst enemy just hisses, and we believe him. We think we have let down everyone around us—even our God—so we spend far too much time brooding and lamenting.

Could it be that all the doing or speculating about whether we're doing enough is the bigger problem?

No more. Knowledge is power. Our Father God knows and sees us hiding behind the curtain with green ink stains all over our hands, and He loves us fully and completely. Just as my friend scooped up her son and asked him not to color mommy's dresses anymore, so too will God correct—but He will forgive you, love you, and even remember your sins no more.

> The LORD is compassionate and gracious,
> slow to anger, abounding in love.
> He will not always accuse,
> nor will he harbor his anger forever;
> he does not treat us as our sins deserve
> or repay us according to our iniquities.
> For as high as the heavens are above the earth,
> so great is his love for those who fear him;
> as far as the east is from the west,
> so far has he removed our transgressions from us.
> As a father has compassion on his children,
> so the LORD has compassion on those who fear him.
> PSALM 103:8-13

How does it make you feel to know that God will take your "green marker moments" and remember them no more?

If He is so quick to forgive, we need to be too, Mom. Thank Him, with a prayer for His willingness to forgive and forget. And then commit to forgive yourself for those mistakes.

Here's the thing, when I bring some of these perceived mega-mistakes up to my children, they look at me like I'm nuts. Most of the areas where I just knew I had scarred them for life are long forgotten by them.

Mom, we waste precious energy that could be spent making memories with our kids. Trust me, your children will not remember the immaculately kept home or that you never served the same meal twice on any given month. They will remember when you got down on the floor and built towers, drew animals with sidewalk chalk, and spent the day blowing bubbles and flying kites. They will also remember the words you spoke and how you spoke them. And they'll remember moments when they "caught" you with your Bible open, soaking up God's Word or bent in prayer.

God knows motherhood is hard. In His divine brilliance, He can use motherhood as a tool to break down our stubborn, hard-headed ways—to seek Him, to draw closer to Him, and to more fully depend on Him. Our days are filled with opportunities to turn to Him, because He is there, waiting to fill us with all that we need.

Here's one example. On a regular basis, I find myself murmuring, *Does anyone even hear me when I speak?* That longing to be heard makes me grouchy and puts me on edge. Could it be that God is using the mundane to guide me into a divine conversation with Him?

Mom, let the following Scriptures speak to your longing to be heard:

> Trust in the LORD with all your heart
> and lean not on your own understanding
> **PROVERBS 3:5**

> So do not fear, for I am with you;
> do not be dismayed, for I am your God.
> I will strengthen you and help you;
> I will uphold you with my righteous right hand.
> **ISAIAH 41:10**

> Humble yourselves, therefore, under God's mighty hand, that he may lift you up in due time. Cast all your anxiety on him because he cares for you.
> **1 PETER 5:6-7**

Share a time when you wanted to be heard by man, but chose to draw close to the Lord, and He provided just what you needed. If you haven't experienced such a time, begin allowing daily time to focus your thoughts on Him.

We have, deep within us as women, a need to be heard. We must be mindful that when that need rises up within us, we are better off going to God with our voices in prayer. Our sister Eve revealed our need to be heard in the garden. She so enjoyed the conversation with the serpent because he listened to her side of the story. Each embellished the story even further, adding to and taking away—just to puff her up and help her to feel heard.

When you feel the need to be heard, see that as a reminder that what your soul is longing for is to be in communion with God, to be heard by Him. Sometimes we just need to be reminded of God's ways and His desire to care for us.

TAKE ACTION

Look up Zephaniah 3:17. As you can see, God delights in you. Spend some time in prayer, asking God to reveal the areas in your life that are "stealing" you away from spending time with Him and the children He has entrusted to you. Then take some time to plan ways you can delight in each member of your family.

Family Member	*Fun Activity*	*When & Where*

DIG DEEPER

There's a Bible story that speaks directly to our female bent to busy ourselves doing for others. Even doing really good things, like preparing a meal for Jesus and friends, can use all our energies for all the wrong reasons. Read Luke 10:38-42.

Are you a Mary or a Martha ... or a little bit of both?

Rewrite here what Jesus said to Martha, replacing your name with hers. How can this encourage you to focus your energy on the right things this week?

HOW DOES YOUR GARDEN GROW?

For the sake of what we've spent the last couple days cultivating in the garden, let's agree to see our homes as a garden—our own little garden of Eden that we are to create for our family. As moms, that is what God has called us to do. Mothers are the nurturers, the nesters, and the ones who cocoon their family from the harsh world.

Moms comfort and soothe us when we are hurt. They guide us when we are lost. They correct us when we are wrong. They show us that things will be OK.

Write down a memory in your life when all you wanted was your mom or motherly figure because you knew she would make it all better.

There are probably deep emotions attached to that memory. As best as you can, share how her safety and care affected your hurt or pain.

Mom, we are the soft place for every member of our family. God fashioned us that way and we need to embrace and revel in that blessed privilege.

Deep in your heart of hearts you know the feelings evoked in you when you remember sweet, precious mom moments with your own mother or motherly figure, grandmother, and with your own precious children. But did you realize there are opportunities for these moments with your kids every single day? Or have you allowed all the to-do's to rob you of what your heart was designed to do—love? There is only one way to put it: Mom, you must make time for your children—and every moment counts.

Anyone who has ever tended a garden knows that a plant cannot grow, bloom, and flourish if it doesn't get the care and nourishment it needs. A plant must also be cared for and protected from weeds and the harsh elements. It's an interesting parallel to raising our children.

In what ways do you know your children need to be cared for by you?

In what areas of life do you know your children need protection from today's fast-paced world? What can you do to better guard them?

Consider the following verses as they relate to your responsibilities as a parent:

> Jesus said to his disciples: "Things that cause people to stumble are bound to come, but woe to anyone through whom they come. It would be better for them to be thrown into the sea with a millstone tied around their neck than to cause one of these little ones to stumble."
> **LUKE 17:1-2**

> Children are a heritage from the LORD,
> offspring a reward from him.
> **PSALM 127:3**

I once heard a pastor make the following statement and it stuck with me. He said, "God decides our encounters; we decide our engagement."[2]

God will give you opportunities to encounter your children every day. But just how are you supposed to engage with them?

I love movies where the story involves transformation in the most unlikely of ways, where through some glorious twist of fate someone begins to see life in a whole new way. Interestingly, the movies to which I am referring are not epic sagas; they are comedies. You know the movies—the ones where a grown-up swaps places with a kid, or a kid is instantly transported to adulthood, and they see and experience the world through the heart and eyes of a kid? My kids love these movies too! Why are we drawn to this recurring story line? For me, it's something about the way life once seen as "ordinary" is transformed into the extraordinary. What was once felt to be a burden in life is reinvented as an opportunity. Life that was once lived with humdrumery and ordinariness is then lived with wonder and a character bursting with curiosity.

A surge of "I can change the world" erupts from the new heart and eyes living out an ordinary life from a new enhanced perspective.

Moms, that's what I want to happen to you! I wish I could trade places with you, and let you see what this mom sees while nearing the empty nest. I want that same transformation to occur in your own hearts and minds that we see in those movies. And it can. It doesn't take a talking head, a birthday wish, or a fortune cookie to cause a transformation.

The closer you get to Jesus, the more you see life His way—that life is about relationship, nurturing, serving, and experiencing the simple. After all, that's what Jesus did. Can you stop long enough to see the world through the eyes of our Savior? The gift of what you're experiencing right now with your children—the joys, struggles, heartaches, messes, and all?

If there is one thing Jesus taught us more than any other, it is to make time for people. Jesus was sent to earth to change the world, yet He didn't rush from task to task, chore to chore ... and His assignment was to save the world. But He knew the world would be saved by starting with the ones closest to Him. He spent time with people, and He modeled for us that every moment counts.

Jesus made it a priority to spend time with God. So can we.

> *What do you notice about Jesus as you read these Scriptures?*
>
> *Matthew 14:23*
> *Mark 1:35*
> *Mark 6:31*
> *Luke 6:12*

Mom, lean in close. This is what this mom of two precious children who are soon to be out on their own wants to tell you: make time. As the "older woman" now, Titus 2:4 directs me to tell you.

> *Write out Titus 2:4.*

Mom, I urge you to love your children through quality time spent with them. The word "love" found the second time in that verse is *philoteknos* in the Greek, and it appears nowhere else in Scripture. It's defined as "motherly love, loving one's offspring or children."[3]

You know what mother love can do? Your baby follows your voice. Your toddler lights up when you walk in a room. Your young child constantly pleads, "Watch me, Mom!" Teens want to process and spend late nights talking with you. (Some mom advice here: when they push back, ignore it, lean in, and keep pursuing your teen.) Your college students seek your advice as they explore, seek, fail, and succeed. It's you they want to hear from. Even your adult children will model your marriage, career choices, and eventually, decisions regarding their own children.

TAKE ACTION

Place your children's names here: _____
are in need of philoteknos *from me, and I am the only one who can provide them with that kind of love.*

Consider all the aspects of motherly love. What are you doing well? What aspect could use some more attention (quality as well as quantity) to better love your kids today? Commit to working on this area until it becomes a habit.

DIG DEEPER

Turn to the New Testament and pick one of the Gospels. Read through a few of the following accounts of Jesus' interaction with those who were a part of His daily life and those He encountered. Then notice the nuisances and patterns of how He made time for, noticed, and cared about others.

Mark 5:21-43
John 4:1-30
John 8:1-11
Luke 7:36-50
Luke 8:40-48

Now spend some time in prayer, asking God if He would help you notice and react more like Jesus to the needs of your family and friends. Also ask Him to reveal what you may have to let go of and say no to in order to have more time to do just that.

DAY 5
FRUIT LADEN

My banana bread is sort of famous where I live, thanks to a recipe compliments of my mother, and her mother, and her mother before her. Making banana bread makes me happy, partly because of the heritage behind it. I remember the first time my kids really paid attention to the bread-making process. They scrunched up their little faces and squealed, "Ew, those bananas are gross!" But by the time I added the flour, sugar, baking soda, butter, and those squishy bananas, we had a delicious mixture of batter that yields the most amazing of sweet breads. Any baker knows that the very best banana bread is made from ripened bananas, and the more ripened the better. Or as my kids would say, "The grosser the better!"

It may be a stretch, but I think we take all the good stuff in our family, add in some rotten parts that help sweeten the batter all the more, and we end up with a most amazing story that is our life.

> *For you, what's the most important element of building a home that can withstand whatever comes against it?*

> *Read Matthew 7:24-27. Then answer the question above again, based on what God says about building a home.*

We all have storms, rotten bananas, and crazy mom days. God uses the trials and triumphs of family life to draw us to Him and give us a common story to share—one that bonds us and brings glory to Him. The mere fact that we get through parenthood and can share sweet memories on the other side gives us a hope for the future.

God can do that.

I do love me some fruit. My favorites are berries—blackberries, raspberries, and straw-berries. For years we lived within a couple miles of a berry patch, and berry picking is actually something I quite enjoy. It's so peaceful, and the hide-and-seek of finding plump, ripe berries keeps me picking away—even in those prickly blackberry bushes!

The Bible has a lot to say about the fruit that should be growing in our homes, and it does not include prickly thorns.

> But the fruit of the Spirit is love, joy, peace, forbearance, kindness, goodness, faithfulness, gentleness and self-control. Against such things there is no law.
> **GALATIANS 5:22-23**

Make a list of the fruit of the Spirit below. Then to the right of each, list ways in which you've exhibited those fruit toward your family during the past week.

How did Jesus say people of God will be recognized (see Matt. 7:16)?

What did Jesus do to the fig tree that didn't bear fruit (see Matt. 21:19)?

Jesus wanted His disciples to see that, as His followers, they needed to not merely "appear" to be religious; their faith needed to have something else attached to it—bearing fruit.

> What good is it, my brothers and sisters, if someone claims to have faith but has no deeds? Can such faith save them? Suppose a brother or a sister is without clothes and daily food. If one of you says to them, "Go in peace; keep warm and well fed," but does nothing about their physical needs, what good is it? In the same way, faith by itself, if it is not accompanied by action, is dead.
> **JAMES 2:14-17**

What does James 2:14-17 reveal that must accompany our faith?

Reflecting on the fruit of the Spirit again, jot down a practical way you will put your faith in action toward a family member this week.

How can you lead your family to bear fruit for those in your circle of influence—at work, at school, and in your community?

TAKE ACTION

Here's what I know. As moms, we regularly do a good job of revealing the fruit of the Spirit toward those we love. Now, we may not always do it perfectly, but my guess is, if you are reading these words and your heart's desire is to be a good mom, you have successes related to each fruit of the Spirit. And you likely excitedly wrote down plans for the week for each family member.

More and more, the notes I get from moms and the conversations we share reveal that moms really are far too hard on themselves. In our minds, even if we are making it a point to show our faith by loving others well, we still seem to falter on giving generously to ourselves. We judge ourselves far too harshly and do not see ourselves the way God sees us. Let's see how you're doing in this area. We'll refer to this as "self-talk."

Once again, write the fruit of the Spirit below. To the right of each, describe ways in which you've exhibited the fruit of the Spirit toward yourself this week—a time when there was positive self-talk.

That's a different animal altogether, isn't it? Being intentional by giving yourself a break and not being too hard on yourself is a bit more of a reach, don't you think?

For any area above where you have nothing written to the right, I encourage you to practice exhibiting that fruit in your self-talk. Realize the words you say to yourself matter. It really is a good idea to give yourself a mental high five every now and then!

> I want my life to be integrated in the one true reality of a God who knows everything about me and desires for me only the good. I want to view all the distractions of my day from the perspective of eternity. I want to abandon myself to a God who can elevate me beyond the tyranny of my self. I will never be free from evil, or from distractions, but I pray that I can be freed from the anxiety and unrest that crowd in with them.
> —Phillip Yancy, *Reaching for the Invisible God* [4]

DIG DEEPER

It is worth noting that while I implore you, as a mom, to be certain your self-talk is positive, it is also important that you guard yourself from pride. After all, it is not you who produces the fruit; it is your Heavenly Father.

Finish the verses from the following Proverbs (NIV).

*"When pride comes, then comes _____,
but with humility comes _____."*
Proverbs 11:2

*"Where there is _____, there is pride,
but wisdom is found in those who take _____."*
Proverbs 13:10

*"Pride goes before _____,
a haughty spirit before a _____."*
Proverbs 16:18

*"Pride brings a person _____,
but the lowly in spirit gain _____."*
Proverbs 29:23

GROUP TIME: HOW CAN I STOP COMPARING MYSELF?

BEAUTIFUL MESS MOMENT

My kids were all under the age of 5, and we were trying to take the treasured Christmas card photo—complete with coordinating outfits, uncomfortable shoes, adorable red hats, and angelic smiling faces. It began well. Smiles. Giggles. Actually, some of the cutest photos we've ever had were taken on this day, but nothing seemed to meet my unrealistic expectations of perfection. My pushing for better and just the right shot made things worse. Eventually, there were tears, frustration, and tantrums.

Finally, it hit me. We were *done*! What was I thinking trying to push my small children to accomplish something most supermodels spend hours or even days trying to get right? I was tired of comparing my kids to others. A perfect photo was not going to cover up the imperfections in our family, in my kids, or in my abilities as a mom. So we sent out the photo of crying children and signed it "With Joy and Love!"

☐ *Who in your life seems to have it all figured out and appears to have it all together? How do you find that you compare yourself to this person?*

DISCUSS

☐ *We discussed this some in the first session, but why do moms put so much pressure on themselves to be perfect and compare their lives with those of others? Why is it in our nature to do this?*

☐ *What are the positive things you can learn from watching and comparing how other moms raise their children and deal with everyday challenges? Give an example of when this happened to you.*

☐

☐ How does it negatively impact you to compare yourself to others?

☐ Read Psalm 139:13-16. What do these verses tell you about how God made you? Write your thoughts and feelings beside each word or phrase.

    Created by God—
    Wonderful—
    God knows you—
    God sees you—

☐ How do you feel when you consider how God created each of us to be unique? What kind of impact does that truth have on you as you continue to compare yourself with others? How does it change your perspective?

☐ What if, instead of being a mom who constantly compared herself with others, you remembered your unique qualities? What if you began to compliment the positives you saw in others that in the past brought envy or feelings of insecurity? What if you became known as the mom who is recognized for how she appreciates people, places, and even the most simple things in life? How would your attitude and your outlook on life change?

☐ If we aren't careful, we'll only see the mess and miss the beauty in life. How have you focused more on the messy part of life in the last month?

☐ What are three steps or actions you might take to focus less on the mess of you and more on the beauty of who God created you to be?

Comparison is a normal part of life. We may never stop comparing ourselves with others. But we can make a conscious effort to control comparing ourselves with others.

WEEK 3
HOW CAN I STOP COMPARING MYSELF?

Have you ever noticed that when we walk into a gathering with other women one of the first things we do is check each other out? We notice her cute skirt and how well her shoes match her top. We notice the designer bag on her shoulder and how slim her waist is. It sometimes seems automatic, the way we're wired to notice the details of someone else—the way she wears her hair, the color of her nail polish, or the smart look of her outfit. Yet the next step I often find myself sliding into is, *She looks so good in those pants. Why can't I stop eating those brownies so my backside could fit into her size?*

This is the danger of comparisons. They make us forget the wonderful things about ourselves and focus on the not-so-good. And when we compare ourselves with someone who looks like we think we should or excels at what we don't, our faults grow even bigger in our own eyes. *She's all of that, and I'm none of that and I never will be.*

God tells me in His Word that "I am fearfully and wonderfully made" (Ps. 139:14). It's sometimes hard to believe this when I step out of the shower dripping wet and catch a full glimpse of my unvarnished and unadorned glory. Does God not know the definition of *beautiful?* He must be mistaken, because there are days when I'm sure I'm anything but. But I'm learning this is Satan's plan, which is the total opposite of what God wants for me. And the same goes for you.

We all compare ourselves to others; it's human nature. But that doesn't mean it's healthy. Why is comparing ourselves to other women so damaging for us? And what are some practical solutions for keeping our eyes on what God says about us? Mom, keep reading.

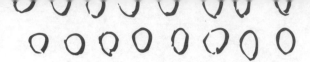

DAY 1
SHE SEEMS SO PERFECT.

When she opened her refrigerator door, I (Sherry) thought, *You have got to be kidding!* The shelves were pristine, with the milk lined neatly against one side, flanked by the bottles of orange and cranberry juice, all on the shelf labeled "Drinks." Everything had its place, in an order that made sense, with the cheeses and lunch meats in their special drawer and the items in the crisper actually looking fresh and crisp. The wild thought flicked across my brain to salute the contents of her refrigerator to see if they would snap to attention and salute back. I sighed as I thought of my fridge at home: an empty milk jug on the middle shelf (Could someone please just throw it away when you've drained the last drop?) and leftovers with good intentions that long ago had lost any semblance of the food they once were. If I had to fix a decent meal for surprise guests who dropped in, I would be hard-pressed with my lack of decent ingredients. I wouldn't want to open the fridge anyway, lest they see the chaos. Joan's refrigerator made me think organized and well-stocked; mine made me feel depressed.

But this was how I often felt when I went to Joan's house. She was so well thought out and put together. She exercised every morning, planned her meals a week in advance, and never seemed flustered or rushed. Her house was beautiful and her closet organized by color. She could find anything in her purse at a moment's notice. I could build a summer house out of dryer lint in the time I've wasted digging in my purse. After spending time with Joan, I often wished I could be like her.

> *With whom do you frequently compare yourself? What is it about that person that makes you feel inadequate?*

> *What do you struggle to like about yourself? How does that relate to the person you've been comparing yourself to?*

I frequently question why someone else's strengths make me notice my weaknesses. I can sing, I can teach a children's class, and I can plan and lead an event, but keep my refrigerator clean and my pantry organized? Nope, I'm a sorry mess. And this is the slippery slope of comparing myself with someone else. No matter what my strengths are, I can always find someone who's even better.

Throughout God's Word, He tells us what He sees when He looks at us: moms full of promise and hearts filled with love, women who have unique gifts and talents that we can each use to make a difference. We may know this in our heads, but it's another thing to really live it. Here's how we can daily let this sink into our hearts.

Thankfulness is really an art form, something to study and learn. As we practice how to really be thankful, we realize it takes our comparing eyes off others and forces us to delight in what God has given us to enjoy. It brings forward a feeling of being blessed, which will shut down our need to nitpick ourselves. When we take time to really be thankful for the lives we lead, that recognition of our blessings will eat up the space we would normally fill with noticing what we don't have or what we're not.

It's taken me a while to realize what I'm really good at and to appreciate its value. How about you? Do you know what your strengths are? Begin by identifying what you're really good at and love doing. Then look for opportunities to use those gifts to bless somebody else. Are you a great cook? Look for opportunities in which bringing a meal could really make someone feel loved and lighten her day. Are you an encourager? A well-chosen word can literally change the way someone feels about herself and turn her day around. Take a new look at what you are gifted at—no matter how small you might think it is—and pour yourself into it.

Make a list of your strengths and passions.

David knew his strengths and used them to his advantage while tending his father's sheep. First Samuel 16:1-13 tells the story of how God chose David to be the next king of Israel. David was the youngest of six older and more impressive brothers, so when Samuel was sent to Jesse's house to choose a future king, David's father didn't even consider calling in his youngest son from the fields where he was tending sheep. Even Samuel, the prophet of God, fell prey to the dangers of comparison by looking at the intelligence, height, or beauty of each man presented before him. So God reprimanded Samuel:

> But the LORD said to Samuel, "Do not consider his appearance or his height, for I have rejected him. The LORD does not look at the things people look at. People look at the outward appearance, but the LORD looks at the heart."
> 1 SAMUEL 16:7

God does not behave like humans. Despite what appearances we see, God sees the motives of others. He knows our true character and if we're willing to obey Him. God created us, and He alone knows the full potential of our strengths.

Young David was faithful to do the work he was asked to do in his family as a shepherd. And for his faithfulness, he was rewarded. David would use his experiences as shepherd throughout his lifetime—to play music for the King (1 Sam. 16:15-23), to slay a giant (1 Sam. 17), while on the run from King Saul (1 Sam. 19), and, ultimately, to lead his people as the king of Israel (2 Sam. 1–1 Kings 2:11).

> *Do the things you dislike about yourself originate from others or from you? When have you allowed human eyes to dictate your view of yourself?*

Let's dig into self-talk a little more. Would you talk to others the way you talk to yourself? Pay attention to that voice in your head; if it's not a nice one, redirect it. Remind yourself of the good stuff—the parts of you that are wonderful (there are lots of them)—and stop yourself when comparisons arise. Begin by relying on verses that will remind you of what God says about you, like these:

> The LORD your God is with you,
> the Mighty Warrior who saves.
> He will take great delight in you;
> in his love he will no longer rebuke you,
> but will rejoice over you with singing.
> **ZEPHANIAH 3:17**

> I praise you because I am fearfully and wonderfully made;
> your works are wonderful,
> I know that full well.
> **PSALM 139:14**

God knows you better than anyone else, and if He declares you delightful just the way you are, then you truly are!

What are the lies that you've bought into about yourself? How do these lies stand up against Zephaniah 3:17 and Psalm 139:14?

What are three positive statements about yourself as a woman, wife, or mom that you know to be true?

Like David, what potential might God see in the strengths you possess? How can you use those abilities to help another mom?

TAKE ACTION

Pick a favorite go-to Scripture to read every day that reminds you how much God loves you. Reflect on it and say to yourself, *God says this is true and it is true despite how I think or feel.*

DIG DEEPER

On a sheet of paper, list the things you don't like about yourself, writing them with a water-soluble marker. As you look at the list, pour water over your sheet and watch as your writing is washed away. Continue to pour water until the sheet is clean. This is how God sees you: "Though your sins are like scarlet, they shall be as white as snow; though they are red as crimson, they shall be like wool" (Isa. 1:18). Can you claim these words as yours?

Spend a few minutes in prayer, seeking what God wants to say to you through your study today.

Write the positive attributes about yourself on a card and put them where you'll see them every day. Read them out loud to yourself.

DAY 2
WHAT DOES GOD SEE WHEN HE LOOKS AT ME?

Mothering is not for the faint of heart. It often feels like a job of sacrifice with little outward reward and reinforcement.

A mom friend of mine recently commented that she wished motherhood involved year-end evaluations and goals. She was joking, but there was truth underlying her words. As a mom of small children, she doesn't often have someone telling her what a good job she is doing. Motivating words to keep us moving forward are powerful, and as moms, sometimes they just don't come often enough.

Recently, my friend left a park play date with a toddler throwing a fit, a wailing baby in her sling, and her two older children bickering in the background. An older mom friend who was observing the situation said, "You're such a good mom." They were simple and yet powerful words for a young mom to grasp, recognizing that her patience, love, and redirection meant something, even in the midst of meltdowns. What mom hasn't felt the weight of a grocery cashier's disapproval as her child throws a tantrum at the checkout?

When have you felt like a mom disaster or failure?

In a moment of sheer discouragement, my friend experienced God's loving voice through another mom's words. The Lord said to her, "You are enough. I entrusted you with these children, and you, as their mom, are enough."

Describe a time when you were encouraged by an onlooker.

It's hard not to feel like a failure when we continually see pictures on Twitter or Instagram of perfectly groomed children looking happy and cheerful in what appears to be a model home—especially when, at that moment, your house is a mess, there's nothing to fix for dinner, and your husband is grumpy.

God sees right through the filters that cloud our vision of ourselves. He sees our struggle to be good enough and instead He gently calls for us to focus our eyes on Him. God planned before the beginning of time that He would give you the children you have, and you are the perfect, beautiful mess for them. You are who they need. Let's look again to 1 Samuel for a better understanding of what God sees in you.

King David is one of the most well-known kings from the Bible (and in history), but his rise to kingship was not typical. As we discussed yesterday, God called His prophet Samuel to go to Bethlehem to pick the new king of Israel from the sons of Jesse. As Jesse paraded his many sons in front of Samuel, the prophet kept thinking, *Surely it's this one—he is smart.* Or, *This one is tall and handsome; it must be him!* But the Lord whispered in Samuel's ear what we often need to hear. Read verse 7 again:

> "Do not consider his appearance or his height, for I have rejected him. The LORD does not look at the things people look at. People look at the outward appearance, but the LORD looks at the heart."
> **1 SAMUEL 16:7**

David had to be brought in from his shepherding duties from the fields. He probably wasn't looking (or smelling) his best, but when God looked at David, He saw the future king of Israel and a man after His own heart.

As you mull the story of how God saw a king when He looked at David when others saw a shepherd boy, consider how the Lord really sees you.

Who do you think God sees when He looks at your mom heart?

Does He see joy? Frustration? Insecurity? A deep desire to be loved and known? Does He see a mom who is overwhelmed? Inadequate? Uncaring? Or does He see a mom who loves her children with all of her heart, a mom who sometimes struggles with anger and frustration, but one who would sacrifice anything for the good of her family?

What fears and feelings of being overwhelmed have you never put into words?

You may think God looks at you and sees failure or disappointment. Perhaps you think He's mad at you because you've made too many mistakes. If you're struggling to see the beauty in yourself—in all your insecurities and flaws—you're failing to see just how much God loves you. Mom, the Bible says that God considers you to be His child.

> I will be a Father to you,
> and you will be my sons and daughters,
> says the Lord Almighty.
> 2 CORINTHIANS 6:18

> See what great love the Father has lavished on us, that we should
> be called children of God! And that is what we are! The reason
> the world does not know us is that it did not know him.
> 1 JOHN 3:1

No matter who you are or what you've done, God loves you. And He wants you to see the beauty within yourself and in your role as a mother. He wants to guide and protect you, and for you to turn to Him with all your struggles and insecurities. Yet God takes it even a step further. When you believe in Him and receive His Son as your Savior, He sees you as a forgiven child, one who will enjoy the inheritance of His eternal kingdom.

> All the prophets testify about him that everyone who believes
> in him receives forgiveness of sins through his name.
> ACTS 10:43

> Everyone who calls on the name of the Lord will be saved.
> ACTS 2:21

When you fully understand how much God loves you, you can see just how valuable and blessed you are.

> *How does being a child of God change the way you view yourself?*
> *How does it affect your view of motherhood?*

Write a prayer of thankfulness to God for all He's given you.

TAKE ACTION

A great way to escape the trap of comparison is to encourage another mom. Think again about when encouraging words have lifted your heart. What was meaningful about these words? How can you give this same experience to another mom? Here are some ideas:

• *Write a letter to another mother, listing everything you're learning from her example as a mom. Try to focus on what you see from her heart rather than outward things. Close the letter by promising to pray for her often. And keep your promise.*

• *Catch a mom by surprise in the grocery store or at the park and encourage her with the words "I love the way you ..." Try to relate it to something you see in her or her children at the moment.*

• *Send a text to another mom to simply say, "I love you, and I'm praying for you right now." Keep your promise to pray.*

DIG DEEPER

King David did nothing to become a king. He didn't hire a campaign manager or a marketing firm to get his name out there. He wasn't being groomed to rule and take over the kingship of Israel. He wasn't even part of his own father's parade of sons before the prophet Samuel! David was the youngest of many sons and was performing his duties as a family shepherd when God led Samuel to Jesse's family. David was just a normal guy doing his family chores with diligence, faithfully completing his tasks. He wasn't extraordinary by human standards, but God saw David as a masterpiece.

Read 1 Samuel 16. Do you think David struggled to see himself as king? What thoughts might he have had about his qualifications?

What do you think of when you picture a masterpiece? How can you begin to picture yourself as God's masterpiece?

DAY 3
HOW DO WE GET OFF TRACK?

Why was she chosen and not me? I felt rotten even wondering this question. She was my friend. She was wonderful and talented, and I loved her. So where in the world were these thoughts coming from? We were getting ready for Easter weekend at our church and our worship pastor was assigning singing parts. My friend was honored to be asked to sing a worship song that she loved and that matched her voice perfectly. Even to this day, I feel miserable that my first thought was *Why didn't they ask me?*

Even when we don't want to travel down the ugly road of petty smallness, we sometimes find ourselves gearing up for the journey. As my grandma used to say, "Sometimes a bad thought will come knocking at your door, but you don't have to invite it in for coffee and a piece of pie!"

How true. I park my thoughts exactly where I choose to park them. I can camp out on delight, or I can ruminate with the ugly stepsisters: envy and jealousy. They aren't really the same, but they sometimes come packaged together in one nasty bundle. Envy is wanting something that somebody else has and is sometimes accompanied by the jealous feeling that it should've been yours to start with. In the case of my talented singing friend, I wanted the opportunity she had gotten, and I felt bad that she would be singing the song that I felt I should be singing. My feelings were compounded by my shame in feeling them in the first place.

But isn't that what Satan does? He confuses the situation with smoke and mirrors and gets our conscience all tied up in knots. He starts with getting our eyes on others and making the good about their lives appear even better. He then makes the good God has given us seem small and insignificant, and he sprinkles in some insecurity and an attitude of entitlement just for good measure.

As moms, this can be especially damaging. We can get our eyes on other moms and begin to wish we had their homes, their perfectly-behaved children, or their family income. This thinking can lead to a deep feeling of discontent that can wreak havoc in our lives.

Now let's look at how jealousy and envy can derail us and how we can get back on track.

We've talked a lot about how David was chosen and seen by God as the new king of Israel long before anyone else would've considered him the next king. After Samuel

anointed David, it was still a long road before David was recognized as king. Saul was the king at the time, and David became an important part of Saul's household. With his musical gifting on the harp and his killing of the giant Goliath, David began to get more attention than Saul. This did not sit well with King Saul, and he allowed his jealousy of David to take root in his heart and flourish.

> So he sent David away from him and gave him command over a thousand men, and David led the troops in their campaigns. In everything he did he had great success, because the LORD was with him. When Saul saw how successful he was, he was afraid of him. But all Israel and Judah loved David, because he led them in their campaigns.
> 1 SAMUEL 18:13-16

Jealousy and envy never have a happy ending. King Saul attempted many ways to discredit and even eliminate David, and none of them worked. In the end, King Saul killed himself by falling upon his own sword in battle.

Jealousy and envy make you miserable. This is part of Satan's evil plan. They creep into your heart when you start comparing your life to others and let feelings of insecurity and entitlement creep in.

Have you seen jealousy and envy at work in your life?

How do you typically respond to those feelings?

A quick antidote is to let your mind steep on how God has blessed you uniquely, even in the small things. Consider these questions to focus on the gifts God has given you both in who you are and in the gifts of your children.

How are your children unique? As a guide, list five things about each of your children that set them apart from other children.

How are you unique as a mom? What things do you particularly enjoy and what are the opportunities that you have had throughout the past year to enjoy them?

What are you most thankful for in your family? What are you most thankful for as a mom?

How has God uniquely blessed your family in the past year? Have you taken time to express your thankfulness to Him?

TAKE ACTION

But if you harbor bitter envy and selfish ambition in your
hearts, do not boast about it or deny the truth.
JAMES 3:14

Discouragement is a major part of parenthood. You try and try again to do the right things, but at times, the end result isn't what you'd like it to be. You're doing the best you can, and someone else just seems to do it all better. Don't let these feelings make you want to quit. God is on your side, and He wants to help you navigate rough waters. When you find yourself struggling with jealous thoughts, you have the choice to let your thoughts ruminate on envy or jealousy, or to surrender them to God.

Write a prayer that surrenders all those feelings of self-doubt to God. Don't hold back. He wants you to be honest with Him, and He is strong enough to handle your concerns.

DIG DEEPER

Read Paul's words from Philippians:

> I am not saying this because I am in need, for I have learned to be content whatever the circumstances.
> **PHILIPPIANS 4:11**

Can you say the same? Increase your contentment level by taking time to list all the things in your life you're thankful for. How long of a list can you make?

THE DANGER OF COMPARISONS

What had I gotten myself into? I wrestled with this thought as I wrapped green and pink party cups in crisp cellophane, each one filled to the brim with suckers and a box of miniature candy hearts. My irritation welled up as I realized I had left out the Valentine's card from all the Room Moms. I would have to go back, untie each bow, stick in the card and start over with the wrapping. I had to admit that I just wasn't good at this. I was the mom on the Room Mom team who didn't get jazzed up that the color of the party cups matched the color of the turtle suckers, or that we had found the perfect matching Valentine's cards that read, "You're turtle-y awesome!"

Don't get me wrong. I loved being a part of my son's class party and experiencing a small part of his fourth-grade days that were zipping by all too fast. But that had nothing to do with why I was now wrapping turtle-themed party favors at 10:00 p.m. It was because Kay, my son's best buddy's mom, did get really jazzed about matching cups, suckers, and cards, so I thought I should too. I had volunteered to buy, assemble, and wrap it all by myself, like some sort of Valentine's Super Mom. Sigh.

This is the slippery slope of comparisons and why it can be so dangerous. We look at other women—other moms, other wives—and think, *I should try harder to be like them.* The underside of that thought, though, is *because I'm not enough.* And then if you're me, the Valentine's Super Mom wanna-be, you start overcompensating for what you think you're not and doing things for the wrong reasons: to prove to anyone who might be watching that you're OK.

I can't help but wonder what God thinks as He watches me spin around in circles, trying to dance to the beat of a thousand different drummers. Surely He sees my exhaustion and contemplates why I'm looking at her and not at the One who made me. He designed me to love to bake, organize the games, and watch with delight as my son exclaimed over the turtle cups that I didn't have to think up or build. He designed Kay for the thinking and building, so together we're a perfect team.

God has brought us into our place and time in the world and connected us with family, friends, and coworkers who complement our strengths. The same was true for a young orphan who became a queen. Let's look at the story of Esther.

The biblical account of how Esther became queen is a beautiful portrayal of God's grace-filled design in our lives. Esther became engaged in a beauty pageant to become the next queen after the previous queen had been exiled.

> The king's personal attendants proposed, "Let a search be made for beautiful young virgins for the king. Let the king appoint commissioners in every province of his realm to bring all these beautiful young women into the harem at the citadel of Susa. Let them be placed under the care of Hegai, the king's eunuch, who is in charge of the women; and let beauty treatments be given to them. Then let the young woman who pleases the king be queen instead of Vashti." This advice appealed to the king, and he followed it.
> **ESTHER 2:2-4**

For Esther, becoming queen would include following her cousin Mordecai's instruction to hide her Jewish heritage and change her name. Talk about pressure!

> Mordecai had a cousin named Hadassah, whom he had brought up because she had neither father nor mother. This young woman, who was also known as Esther, had a lovely figure and was beautiful. Mordecai had taken her as his own daughter when her father and mother died. When the king's order and edict had been proclaimed, many young women were brought to the citadel of Susa and put under the care of Hegai. Esther also was taken to the king's palace and entrusted to Hegai, who had charge of the harem. She pleased him and won his favor. Immediately he provided her with her beauty treatments and special food. He assigned to her seven female attendants selected from the king's palace and moved her and her attendants into the best place in the harem. Esther had not revealed her nationality and family background, because Mordecai had forbidden her to do so. ... Now the king was attracted to Esther more than to any of the other women, and she won his favor and approval more than any of the other virgins. So he set a royal crown on her head and made her queen instead of Vashti.
> **ESTHER 2:7-10,17**

It's easy for us to look at the superficial elements of the story of Esther and think, *She has it made. She just won the royal jackpot! Twelve months of beauty treatments, seven female attendants, and her own suite of rooms in the castle doesn't sound like a bad deal.* But if we take a closer look, we'll see another side to the story.

Esther suddenly became rivals for the king's attention with the other candidates for queen. Imagine being sequestered for 12 months of beauty treatments to be polished and trained. It was likely a life of loneliness for Esther as she hid who she was—even her name—and wondered how she compared to all the other women vying for the new role of queen. Did she wonder if she measured up? Did she look around at the other potential queens and wish her hair was a little glossier, or her intellect a little sharper? Did Esther believe she was capable of fulfilling God's incredible plan for her life?

The same goes for us. It's far too easy to compare ourselves to other moms and think they have it made. We never truly know what another person's life is like, and it's an absolute fact that we all have flaws.

God created beautiful you—with your untidy pairing of imperfections and unique strengths—to be your child's mother. He knew before time began the little lives He would place into your care, and you—yes, you—are exactly the mother God intended for your children, flaws and all.

> *How do you feel when you see another mom who is good at something you're not? Do you feel pressure to try to get better?*

> *Are you comfortable saying no to things that you don't feel called to do? Why or why not?*

TAKE ACTION

Comparing yourself to other mothers and your children to their children isn't always a negative thing. If seeing someone else at her best encourages you to learn how to better manage the things God entrusted to you, then the comparison is good. If it encourages you to learn and grow in good ways, thank God for showing you those positive observations.

> *Have you ever had an experience in which this was true? What did you learn?*

Is there a specific parenting skill you wish you were better at? Instead of comparing yourself, what can you do to improve in that area?

Now let's look at the flip side. Consider the many strengths you have that others don't.

Each one should test their own actions. Then they can take pride in themselves alone, without comparing themselves to someone else.
GALATIANS 6:4

What burdens do your friends and family carry?

How do you—or could you—help them with those burdens, using your own gifts?

DIG DEEPER

Learning about yourself and finding out your specific strengths can help you to better appreciate your uniqueness and use those gifts for God. There are many great books and self-assessments available to help you do this. Consider using one of these:

☐ *Work through the six-week study* Understanding Spiritual Gifts *by Kay Arthur and BJ Lawson (LifeWay, 2010).*

☐ *Take a free spiritual gifts assessment and explanation available from LifeWay. Go to www.lifeway.com and search under "Articles" for the "Spiritual Gifts Assessment Tools."*

☐ *Take a professional personality profile, such as the DISC Test (www.thediscpersonalitytest.com) or the Myers Briggs MBTI Personality Type test (www.myersbriggs.org).*

☐ *Talk to those who know and love you. Ask them what strengths they see in you and how they have experienced help from your unique abilities.*

DAY 5
ARE YOU RUNNING ON EMPTY?

"What did you have for breakfast today?" My doctor tapped impatiently on her clipboard as she waited for my reply. I was stalling because I knew I didn't have a good answer. I had come to see her because I was generally feeling lousy. I was tired not long after I woke up in the mornings. At night, I was restless and not sleeping well. I was exhausted by afternoon. I thought she'd want to talk about what we (and by "we," I mean "she") could do to help me sleep better, but she decided to start with a different direction. Breakfast? I often thought about it, but it usually didn't make it into my mouth.

What followed was a rather long discourse on the importance of paying attention to what my body needed and how I wasn't paying attention to how I was forcing my body to run on empty. I thought back to the numerous days when, by mid-morning, I had run out of steam, feeling like I couldn't go one more step. She said, "You think breakfast is just about your morning, but it sets the course for the whole day."

How often do you feel yourself running on empty? What most often leaves you feeling drained?

An empty tummy is a relatively easy fix, as my doctor pointed out. "Plan ahead with a quick protein-packed breakfast and tuck some granola and fruit in your bag for a mid-morning snack." Breakfast is one thing, but what about other areas in your mom life where you might be running on empty?

Jesus knew about the dangers of running on empty. There were great moments in Jesus' life when He slipped away to refuel His heart and soul. In Matthew 4, "Jesus was led by the Spirit into the wilderness" where He focused on the temptations that Satan would throw his way (v. 1). In Luke 6, Jesus went off to the mountains and "spent the night praying to God" before He chose His disciples (v. 12). In Matthew 14, Jesus "withdrew by boat privately to a solitary place" so He could lean into the presence of God and grieve the loss of His friend John the Baptist (v. 13). He wasn't just getting away from people; He was refueling and recharging so He could better minister to the people.

Once queen, Esther faced a dilemma that placed the lives of many men, women, and children squarely on her shoulders. Her uncle Mordecai informed her of a plot to kill all the Jews in Susa simply because they were Jews. Esther's first (and very human) reaction was fear. She could be sentenced to death for going into the king's chambers without his summons, but her uncle stressed the importance of her courage:

> When Esther's words were reported to Mordecai, he sent back this answer: "Do not think that because you are in the king's house you alone of all the Jews will escape. For if you remain silent at this time, relief and deliverance for the Jews will arise from another place, but you and your father's family will perish. And who knows but that you have come to your royal position for such a time as this?"
> ESTHER 4:12-14

Esther stopped questioning and fretting, recognizing her unique position to change the course of history. Mordecai encouraged Esther to look beyond her abilities, beyond her fear, to see God in the circumstances. Before she drew up plans or began to garner allies, Esther stopped everything and led her fellow Jews in fasting for three days.

> Then Esther sent this reply to Mordecai: "Go, gather together all the Jews who are in Susa, and fast for me. Do not eat or drink for three days, night or day. I and my attendants will fast as you do. When this is done, I will go to the king, even though it is against the law. And if I perish, I perish." So Mordecai went away and carried out all of Esther's instructions.
> ESTHER 4:15-17

Queen Esther knew she could not move forward on an empty tank. With lives depending on her, Esther took time to pause and refuel. She took her eyes off herself and placed them onto God, the One who could help her change the course of history and save the lives of her people. And in case you don't know or remember the story, Esther's petition to the king, under God's leadership, worked. She saved her people and "there was joy and gladness among the Jews, with feasting and celebrating" (Esth. 8:17).

Mom, you face tough things every day—pressures, losses, loneliness, overstimulation, fatigue, and huge decisions. Little lives are counting on you to guide them. I'm not tapping my pencil impatiently like a doctor waiting for your answer, but I'd like you to truly ponder this next question.

Do you try to face all that's before you as a mom while running on empty?

Just as a protein-packed breakfast fuels your body for the day, times of solitude and space to hear from God will fuel your mom heart. If you find yourself struggling with comparisons that make you question your worth or value as a mom, it might be because your heart is craving to hear God's voice above all the others. You might think your quiet time with God is just a good "Christian girl" thing to do. No, your times of solitude and silence away with God set the course for your life as a woman, wife, and mother—whatever your particular roles may be.

When you're feeling depleted and weary in life or in mothering, where do you turn? Do you seek comfort in food, refuge in TV, or respite in something else?

How can you train yourself to automatically turn to your Heavenly Father for what you need?

TAKE ACTION

So we fix our eyes not on what is seen, but on what is unseen,
since what is seen is temporary, but what is unseen is eternal.
2 CORINTHIANS 4:18

Consider your daily life. Where can you carve out an hour to spend with God? (Are you laughing right now?) Do you have 30 minutes or even 5 minutes?

Mom, don't fret. Start wherever you can by scheduling time for prayer and contemplation with God every day. Find a quiet place to be still and pour out your weary heart to Him. Then ask Him what He wants to say to you. This moment is not about words; it's about being open to God's love for you. Close your eyes and imagine His presence alongside you. Mom, He has been there all along!

DIG DEEPER

Find an hour when you can focus on hearing from God. Read through the apostle Paul's prayer in Ephesians below as though he is speaking directly to you.

For this reason I kneel before the Father, from whom every family in heaven and on earth derives its name. I pray that out of his glorious riches he may strengthen you with power through his Spirit in your inner being, so that Christ may dwell in your hearts through faith. And I pray that you, being rooted and established in love, may have power, together with all the Lord's holy people, to grasp how wide and long and high and deep is the love of Christ, and to know this love that surpasses knowledge—that you may be filled to the measure of all the fullness of God. Now to him who is able to do immeasurably more than all we ask or imagine, according to his power that is at work within us, to him be glory in the church and in Christ Jesus throughout all generations, for ever and ever! Amen.
EPHESIANS 3:14-21

Now read through the prayer again, making a note of each thing Paul prays that his readers will experience.

Go back over the list a final time, asking God to make each promise real to you. Sit in silence and listen for God's response. Write what you hear Him saying to you.

GROUP TIME: HOW DO I PRIORITIZE MY BUSY LIFE?

BEAUTIFUL MESS MOMENT

One year while on vacation, we came upon a giant maze made of plank-board fencing that my children were very excited about trying. They were convinced they could zip right through the thing. My husband went in with them while I stood high above them on the platform to watch and take photos. How did it go? Well, let's just say they overestimated their prowess at avoiding dead ends. At some point, they acquiesced and allowed Dad to lead them out of the maze. When they joined me on the platform watching others, they were amazed at their new perspective on what previously seemed like more than they could handle. Their older, wiser father and those from up above on the platform knew some things my kids didn't, and they had to trust those who knew more—even when they thought they had it all figured out.

□ *How would life be different if God took away all of your problems? What can you do to remind yourself that God is with you in the good and in the bad?*

DISCUSS

□ *How often do you feel like you're caught in a maze and there's no way out? Is it a daily occurrence, or more of a monthly or seasonal cycle?*

□ *How does our striving for more add to that feeling of being thrown into a maze?*

□ *Life has its problems, and some are unavoidable. What are your greatest challenges today when you think about your problems?*

Sometimes we can add to our problems by worrying about tomorrow. We imagine, *What might happen if … ?* We think about all the possibilities of the things that could go wrong. Now imagine getting up each day and allowing that day to care for itself instead of worrying or striving for tomorrow.

Read Matthew 6:34. Are you wondering how you are going to accomplish that? Now go back and read verse 33, and take a deep breath.

The Creator of the universe knew that we impatient humans need to be reminded to just relax and live today fully. So much of the time we get caught up in all the tasks and responsibilities that we forget about the relationships. We let the laundry, dishes, email, work, and school projects infringe upon the time we might spend with others. We get the items checked off the to-do list, but our relationships get out of balance.

   □ *Why is it such a struggle for many moms to relax and live fully in the moment?*

   □ *What are some of the worries and hindrances that cause moms to rush forward, looking ahead and filling their schedules?*

   □ *How important is it for your family (or those who live together in your household) to slow down and avoid worrying about tomorrow?*

   □ *What are the challenges with thinking about the future that affect your family the most?*

Write down Matthew 6:33-34 on a note card, and put it somewhere you'll see it all week. Do at least one thing this week to slow your family down and just spend time together, making memories and loving each other.

WEEK 4

HOW DO I PRIORITIZE MY BUSY LIFE?

Mr. Smith arrived home late from work, sees Mrs. Smith's car in the driveway, and pauses with a smile. Mr. Smith is so looking forward to a night in his beautiful, comfy, cozy home, relaxing and loving his family. As Mr. Smith enters, he notices an eerie silence. Before his curious eyes, he doesn't see the comfy, cozy that just moments before was dancing through his mind. What he sees is chaos and mess. Literally nothing seems to be in place—it's as if the upstairs kids' bedrooms threw up on the downstairs family room and kitchen. Mr. Smith rushes upstairs, finds his beloved wife sitting up in bed, reading. When he asks, "What's going on? Is everything OK? What have you been doing?" Mrs. Smith smiles, explains that the kids just left for a sleepover at Grandma's, and sweetly replies, "Well, I didn't do what I usually do when I'm at home." With that Mrs. Smith cocks her eyebrow and gets back to her reading.

It's a constant battle to keep up with the mess day in and day out. And it certainly is enough to drive any mom bonkers once she begins to wonder if any of it even matters. We've likely all heard and contemplated the definition of insanity: doing the same thing over and over again, expecting different results.

The goal of motherhood isn't achieved in the immediate; we must look to long-term results. Yet in the thick of it, we often feel like all we're doing is wasting time.

How do we manage time when we feel like what we're doing isn't producing the desired effect? Or perhaps the better question is this: Does God think what we're doing is productive and worthy?

Deep breath, Mom. Let's dig in to understand motherhood from God's perspective.

I LOVE BEING A MOM, BUT BEING A MOM MAKES ME CRAZY!

There's this old chair in my kitchen. When I (Tracey) sit in it, my children seemingly disappear. It became "my" chair out of desperation. On one of those particularly I-am-going-to-lose-my-mind sort of days, I went over to that wooden chair, sat down, clinched my jaw, and raised my hands to begin slamming shut imaginary doors. I distinctly recall curious children looking at me silently (it was working already), with their wheels churning: "What are you doing, Mom?" To which I replied, "I can't hear you. I can't speak to you." Thankfully they were young enough to have great imaginations, so just go with me here, because they did. Their curiosity was piqued, and their crazy-making abated: "What do you mean you can't hear me?"

"I'm in my invisible chair," I replied. "When I sit here, that means mom is off-limits. So don't talk to me and stay out of trouble."

Their little eyes narrowed, and it was as if a seed had just been planted in their minds—a "my mom needs something that doesn't involve me" bit of knowledge.

When being a mom gets the best of me, I sit in that chair, take deep breaths, and plead with God: *Why is this so hard? Help me, please!* He listens, soothes, redirects, and the mom God intended me to be is reminded of the importance of my role. That wooden chair has become my sanctuary because God meets me there.

Sometimes being a mom feels like it requires too much. However, despite all our responsibilities, God expects us to give ourselves fully to raising children. He has a plan for our children, and that plan includes us moms—in a big way.

Mom, all that you do for your family, you're doing for God. There's a verse that illustrates this well, one I consider to be the "mom verse" of all time.

> Whatever you do, work at it with all your heart, as
> working for the Lord, not for human masters.
> **COLOSSIANS 3:23**

Rewrite that verse, but replace all the pronouns with the word "I" or "my." Then make this your prayer for the rest of this week.

There are still times when being a mom makes us want to throw our hands up, scream, and contemplate running away. I can even remember hearing my own mother say, "One of these days I'm just going to run away!" So what do we do when we're overwhelmed?

Back in week 2, day 1, we explored our inherent desire to seek refuge. Flip back to page 38 and remind yourself where you're supposed to go for refuge.

> *Has there been a time since that study of refuge when you sought God rather than a counterfeit? Explain.*

During real-life turmoil, or even just a particularly bad day, we need to be inclined to seek God and His perspective, which is always best. For every mom this seeking is different, but for me it's that wooden chair of pretend invisibility.

> *Identify a place and time you could set aside to seek refuge and spend time in prayer. If you already have a spot, evaluate what's working and what's not.*

If I may suggest, Mom, the most valuable commodity you have right now with your children—besides your relationship with God—is time. It might be hard to see, but very soon they will be grown and gone. So it's important to manage well those small moments that quickly become weeks, months, and years. Think about managing time from a biblical perspective.

> From the ends of the earth I call to you,
> I call as my heart grows faint;
> lead me to the rock that is higher than I. ...
> Then I will ever sing in praise of your name
> and fulfill my vows day after day.
> **PSALM 61:2,8**

This is a request for God to grab us in our lowly state and lift our eyes to see life from His eternal point of view. God knows the whole of our lives and the future of our kids' lives, and He can give us direction here and now. What we do in daily moments matters, and God knows what it will ultimately mean in the lives of our children.

As a mom, sometimes every day begins to look the same and headway seems a distant dream. Yet when we turn to God for our strength each day—and sing praises for who He is and what He has done—our days are infused with confidence in Him and who we are because of Him.

Considering the beautiful mess moments of your life, describe a typical night at your home.

As you consider God's perspective of the moments in your home, how might His view differ from your description?

If you see room for improvement, what would you like an average night at your house to look like going forward? Pray, asking God to help you move in this direction.

TAKE ACTION

We tend to lose sight of the end goal while we're in the thick of something. If day after day "momness" has you overwhelmed, and you're wondering if you're wasting a perfectly good mind, then find yourself a mom mentor. Look for someone with kids older than yours whom you can spend time with, learn from, and go to when you want to run away—when the "invisible chair" is being frequented far too often.

Make a list of moms you admire who have children older than yours.

Pray about which of these moms you might invite over for tea or coffee. You may find she has been waiting for a call!

DIG DEEPER

The same statement has been on my refrigerator for more than 15 years: "Do not let the ordinary seem so important that it pushes Jesus out of the way." Put another way, the ordinary of our lives can lull us into complacency and prevent us from experiencing God's extraordinary moments.

How would you define "ritual"? Do you primarily live your life in ritual or in relationship?

A friend once explained to me that her spouse had been part of a religion so full of ritual that it lost all meaning. But once he began having a relationship with God, his life became so much fuller. He anticipated what God was going to do through him. This same ritualistic pattern can form in our own homes. We can become so distracted by following a rote pattern that we fail to recognize we're becoming increasingly unrelational. This could include anything from everyone being on-the-go too much, to having meals in front of the television, to family members spending evenings doing their own thing in different parts of the home, and so forth.

List some patterns in your home that have caused your family to be less relational.

Read Romans 12:1-2. Regarding everyday life, what does this verse say to you?

How can you change the patterns listed above to have more relationship-building moments in your home?

DAY 2
I CAN'T DO THIS.

Is motherhood requiring more than you thought you would have to give? You're not alone. I distinctly remember, while in labor on the way to the hospital, when I turned and looked at my husband and said in complete sincerity, "I don't want to do this anymore. I can't do this. I don't want to do this." And he looked at me, eyes wide, and said, "It's a bit too late for that now." It was the first of many times I've thought, *I can't do this.*

Let's face it, as moms we do a whole lot. And in the process, we're getting a bit frazzled— OK, maybe more than a bit. I've always been fond of the phrase "Keep the main thing, the main thing," and I do believe that's especially true of motherhood.

There are many things you're equipped to do, you've learned to do, you've studied to do, or that you're required to do. However, as a mom, there's one thing you were created to do—and the Almighty created you for it when you became a mother. That's deep, albeit repetitive. But think about it. Either life came from you or, through a series of God-ordained circumstances, you were given a life that God planned for you. In both instances, the same God who created life and breath handed you a life to prepare for living out His purposes.

Have you ever sat and really looked at your kids and realized the potential God has gifted you with? I hope you savor the reality that what you do as a mom really, really matters. Every age and every stage in a child's life is important, and God intends you to be an integral part of each. Something that essential needs to be a top priority. A glorious priority. So regardless of what's packed into your day, there's one basic element that must be a priority: making time for your kids. Will this make it hard on you? Yes. But parenting was never meant to be easy. Parents are endowed with children by their Creator to strengthen their legacy and build His kingdom.

> Be very careful, then, how you live—not as unwise but as wise,
> making the most of every opportunity, because the days are evil.
> Therefore do not be foolish, but understand what the Lord's will is.
> **EPHESIANS 5:15-17**

> *How can parents be foolish with their children? In what ways have*
> *you been foolish as a parent, specifically in time management?*

Reflect on how you prioritize time spent with your kids. Then pray, asking God to help you understand what His will is in this area.

For significantly more than a decade, my husband has led us to create the Eyster Family Action Plan every year during Christmas break. Because he's a business leader, he understands the importance of long-range planning, and thankfully, he has made that a part of our family life. Without it, I may never have recognized the illusion of permanence that parents believe—parenting up close must be done with purpose.

Write down the names and current ages of each of your kids. Then list their ages in five years and in ten years.

Child's Name/Age   *Age in 5 Years*   *Age in 10 Years*

If you're like me, looking at your children's ages on paper will likely make you gasp. And that time will pass faster than you can even imagine.

Here's a basic truth any parent of older kids can tell you: If you do not intentionally choose to be a part of your children's lives in the growing years, you'll lose the privilege of speaking into their lives when they become tweens, teens, and young adults.

Many years ago, my husband and I identified this as building "relational equity" with our kids. We watched those older than us who had great relationships with their teens and inquired about their secrets whenever we could. There was an amazing pattern that evolved. Parents who spent real time with their children—making memories, participating and interacting with their kids in the small things—had tight relationships with their kids as they got older. The importance of that bonding meant that when their tweens and teens were inundated with the world and the "big things" they had to contemplate, they would listen to Mom and Dad, because they had a relationship with Mom and Dad. Your children will be influenced; don't you want a large part of that influence to be from you? Again, God decides our encounters with our children, and we decide our engagement.

You must build relational equity every day with your children in the small things—such as eating at the table together, playing games together, playing at the park together, working on homework together, doing chores together, reading bedtime stories together, and chatting at the end of the day together.

> *Circle the word that kept showing up in the last paragraph. How much is that word a part of your day now?*

> *What other things can you and your children do together that you're not doing as a family now?*

Recently, I was on the phone with a young mom who was asking me how she was going to keep her 2- and 3-year-olds from becoming wild teenagers. This is a question posed to me often. Of course we all must pray, but a very practical, proven method of influence over anyone is relationship. And guess what? There are no shortcuts in relationships; they take time. There are also no guarantees. At some point your kids will make their own decisions, but what you want is for them to be eager for your input and that of other godly adults. So time together simply must be how you do life.

You likely seek daily to understand the ways of God, live them out, and teach them to your children. And you already know how hard it is to hear God's voice above a world clamoring for your attention. Can you even begin to imagine how much harder it is for your children to hear God's voice? You have the privilege of guiding them to hear Him. If you continue to seek God's ways in His Word, you'll be equipped to daily teach your children—and that can be done best when your relationship with them is strong.

TAKE ACTION

> *Read 2 Timothy 3:16. What do Paul's words say to you about parenting?*

God wants to teach you, and then He desires for you to teach your child. Trust me, your ability to teach your children what God breathes into you will be received more readily if they have a relationship with you.

And realize, it's never too late. All children long to matter to their parents regardless of their age, so no matter the past, start now, be intentional, and make time for your kids—just to be with them and to do what they enjoy doing. Enter their worlds and listen to them through all the crazy phases of growing up. Your children's ability to hear you is born out of you making time to listen to them.

DIG DEEPER

Now let's try another exercise. Write the names of each of your kids and how the things of this world will try to influence them in the future.

Child's Name	5-Year Influencers	10-Year Influencers

Where do you see the biggest negative influence in your kids' daily lives? How can you and your children's father combat that danger with your time?

What might you need to let go of to have more time with your kids? Realize it might be a very good thing, but for a time, God may be calling you to step away to spend time with your kids.

What other godly adult could you encourage to spend more time with your child? Ask God to further reveal mentors for your children.

SLOW DOWN AND ENJOY TODAY.

If God knew I was the right mama for these kids living under my roof, then why is it sometimes so very hard? And why do I find myself pushing toward the finish line instead of enjoying the race? Therein lies the problem. Motherhood is not a race with a finish line. Motherhood is a life with a destiny. And a certain little turtle in the fable of the "Tortoise and the Hare" taught us that slow and steady not only wins, it allows enjoyment during the journey.

The beauty of choosing to live every day "on purpose" is that you do find purpose in your days. Instead of striving to do more, you slow down and intentionally choose to spend each day enjoying what's right there in front of you.

Have you ever watched one of God's creatures doing what God created it to do? It is mesmerizing. Every spring we watch a pair of birds build a nest in the corner of our carport. Just outside our kitchen window we can see such care taken to build those nests. Once the chicks arrive, we watch the attentive care lavished on those little birds day after day. Here's the thing—we become riveted. We are invested in those birds. Every day we are at that kitchen sink, looking out the window to make sure all is well with Mr. and Mrs. Chirp and their chicks.

Mom, sometimes we need to reevaluate our lives and sift out the things that keep us from living intentionally. We need reminders to live each day intentionally, concerning ourselves with what lies before us today. Let's look at Matthew 6.

> [25]Therefore I tell you, do not worry about your life, what you will eat or drink; or about your body, what you will wear. Is not life more than food, and the body more than clothes? [26]Look at the birds of the air; they do not sow or reap or store away in barns, and yet your heavenly Father feeds them. Are you not much more valuable than they? [27]Can any one of you by worrying add a single hour to your life? [28]And why do you worry about clothes? See how the flowers of the field grow. They do not labor or spin. [29]Yet I tell you that not even Solomon in all his splendor was dressed like one of these. [30]If that is how God clothes the grass of the field, which is here today and tomorrow is thrown into the fire, will he not much more clothe you—you of little faith? [31]So do not worry, saying, "What shall we eat?" or "What shall we drink?" or "What shall we wear?" [32]For the pagans run after all these things, and

your heavenly Father knows that you need them. ³³But seek first his kingdom and his righteousness, and all these things will be given to you as well. ³⁴Therefore do not worry about tomorrow, for tomorrow will worry about itself. Each day has enough trouble of its own.
MATTHEW 6:25-34

Through this passage, what is God saying to you about your life and your family?

You know, those birds in my carport are not striving, nor do they have to accomplish something for me to be interested in them. Yes, we need to provide for our families, but reread verse 32. Now underline the action verb in that sentence. God knows what you need to survive, but He does not want you to "run" after it.

Instead, what does God say we should do in verse 33? What will happen as a result?

What's the difference between working to provide for your family and striving after worldly things—appearances, possessions, status, and so forth?

God sees, He knows, He is invested, and He loves you and your family. Take the pressure off you, because God does not want you striving. He wants you to seek Him and His will.

What's one thing you and your family can do this week to "seek first his kingdom and his righteousness"?

Sadly, sometimes we moms get in such a rush that we're not enjoying each season of motherhood. Why have we all gotten in such a hurry?

Reflecting on the past, describe some instances when you were pushing and rushing instead of enjoying the moment.

Now describe a sweet memory with your kids that you savor and recognize will never come again because your kids have grown older.

Those wonderful, irreplaceable memories of days gone by will happen over and over and over, if you allow them to. Rushing through your days, striving to reach the "next thing" in your child's day, and even in your child's life, robs you and your child of the growth that is designed to be achieved in each phase.

All this rushing about, could be a cleverly placed distraction that keeps moms from doing the very thing God created them to do—daily nurturing, instruction, and training up a child in the way he or she should go.

Write Proverbs 22:6 below, replacing the word "child" with the names of your children.

What does daily nurturing, instruction, and training up look like to you?

If we rush through our days without looking for opportunities to instruct, we end up in a crazy cycle of stress. We end up working feverishly to grow our kids up—fast. Instead of training up our kids, we actually ramp up our own stress levels. Instead of going with the rhythm of life—even with the flow of the day—we're pushing to get to a preconceived finish line. Daily.

With every new goal created, there's pressure to reach that goal. Don't get me wrong: goals should be set and made, but not goals that are causing you to push your children into growing up. There seems to be a race to feed our kids solid food, get them potty-trained, get them into a preschool, get them reading, get them into organized sports, get them trained as classical musicians, and get them enrolled in college. OK, maybe I skipped a few steps there, but really—so many of us are living life for the "next" goal instead of being present in the moment. None of the aforementioned are bad things, Mom; just take the pressure off yourself and your kids to get things achieved.

What goals are you racing to achieve that you need to slow down to enjoy?

TAKE ACTION

Mom, please cut yourself some slack. Balancing it all is hard. But what if you stopped fretting over your time-management skills and concentrated more on your people skills? If you're effectively caring for the needs of the people in your life, the amount of time you have won't stress you nearly as much. When you boil it down to the essentials, your family, your work, and your volunteerism are all about meeting needs. Tune into the needs and not the clock.

What would tuning into the needs of those around you instead of the clock mean for your daily life?

I'll give you two examples. Here's one of those nights when you need to work but your child needs time with you: "Buddy, my boss really needs this report. So let's get your spelling words and you sit up here next to me. While you work on your spelling words for your teacher, I will work on this report for my boss."

Here's another idea. When rush and anger start to well up in you, make the decision to turn it around and be a silly mom. Let's say you're trying to get out the door, and no one is cooperating. Your frustration level is at an all-time high. Instead of screaming, "Get your shoes on those feet and that hat on your head *now!* We're going to be late!" go with, "Get those shoes on your head and that hat on your feet pronto. We have places to go and people to see!" Then put a hat on your feet and start laughing. Usually if you can diffuse the situation with silliness, the mood shifts and kids become more cooperative.

Let's agree right now to soak up and enjoy each stage of a child's life instead of pushing to get to the next one. Oh, and start trying the silly thing too!

DIG DEEPER

If your daily motivation is "What's next?" in your child's life, consider changing that paradigm to "What's now?" in your child's life.

> The LORD has done it this very day;
> let us rejoice today and be glad.
> **PSALM 118:24**

List several reasons you have to "rejoice" and "be glad" today.

Now write down the name of each of your family members. Next to each name, list a way you could spend individual time with him or her this month doing something fun.

God isn't expecting perfection from you. No one is a perfect mom, but you're the perfect mom for the kids God has entrusted to you. And when you approach that role with the wonder and attentive care it requires, you'll find much peace and joy in simply doing what you were made to do: be the mom. And in the process, being intentional in each season of life will enable you to care for your "chicks" and be ready, without regrets, when the time comes for your babies to leave the nest.

DAY 4
GOT ARROWS?

I've always been supportive of the activities my children enjoy. Some are more exciting than others, but all can serve a purpose to teach something, if you look for it. There's always more than meets the eye.

My daughter was on an archery team in high school, and she gained a new appreciation for the ability to be cool, calm, and collected even under pressure. Regardless of the endorphins surging through her body, she had to grasp an arrow, place it on her bow, breathe slowly, and launch that arrow straight toward its target. Archery is certainly one sport where adrenaline can work against you if you don't learn control.

However, no matter how calm she was, if she did not have arrows that were designed to do what they were supposed to do or that had not been taken care of properly, things didn't turn out well. No matter how well she launched her arrows, an ill-prepared or mishandled arrow did not hit its intended target. Period.

> Children are a heritage from the LORD,
> offspring a reward from him.
> Like arrows in the hands of a warrior
> are children born in one's youth.
> **PSALM 127:3-4**

Children are said to be three things in these verses. List them below.

Beside each of those words above, describe what wells up inside of you when you see your kids in that way.

God highly values our children, and we should too. As parents fully grasp how God values their children, it empowers them to establish the priorities necessary to best prepare their children for adulthood.

Too many in our culture see children as an interruption or distraction when actually they are our greatest calling. We must see the importance of preparing our arrows as God directs, and protecting our arrows from the patterns of this world, in order that they can hit their intended target—bringing glory to God.

What qualities do you want to develop in your children? What things can you do to intentionally grow these characteristics?

TAKE ACTION

As you consider how God may want you to prepare your arrows, realize you should get help from others. You can't do it all by yourself, and you're not the only person who can influence your children for God's best. Many godly adults can help influence and shape the people your children are becoming.

Often, when we gather together in large groups, we tend to separate our families and hang out with people our own age. But kids need to be around and learn from all generations. Parental advice reinforced by other adults can sink even deeper into our children's hearts and minds.

Make a list of folks in the following categories who you would like to influence your kids. Then take some steps to make that happen.

5-10 Years Older   A Generation Older   Two Generations Older

How can you encourage your children to take an interest in older generations?

It's also essential that our kids spend time with older Christian kids. That way they can closely see that good life choices lead to successful and fulfilled young adults. My own kids were part of small groups that were led by young adults and they went to a Christian camp annually where they were influenced by amazing college students who were chasing after God but who had crazy, clean fun—something both my children aspire to now!

Beside each verse below, write what the Bible has to teach us about how the company we keep can influence us.

Walk with the wise and become wise,
for a companion of fools suffers harm.
PROVERBS 13:20

Do not make friends with a hot-tempered person,
do not associate with one easily angered,
or you may learn their ways
and get yourself ensnared.
PROVERBS 22:24-25

Do not be misled: "Bad company corrupts good character."
1 CORINTHIANS 15:33

In the name of the Lord Jesus Christ, we command you, brothers and sisters, to keep away from every believer who is idle and disruptive and does not live according to the teaching you received from us.
2 THESSALONIANS 3:6

DIG DEEPER

If you show kids the right pattern to follow and they get glimpses of what life can be like, they will want the same for themselves. The primary pattern my husband and I have tried to teach and show our kids has always been "Love God, love others" (see Matt. 22:37-40). That's what matters most. We simply have not patterned "Make money, be successful." I know that's counter to our culture, but we're following what Jesus taught.

What patterns are you teaching and showing your kids?

Sometimes I feel as though I'm crafting my arrows with a dull knife. I fret that I'm going to mess them up so they will not hit their targets. God is able, but we must go to Him to have the wisdom to teach our kids, and that takes time.

Read Ephesians 6:17. How does it describe the Word of God?

Read Hebrews 4:12. How does it describe the Word of God?

Now let's go back to the Scripture we used to start today's time together.

> Like arrows in the hands of a warrior
> are children born in one's youth.
> **PSALM 127:4**

Our children are like _____.

Stop and think about the symbolism here, Mom. God sees your children as arrows—arrows parents are to craft—and He has given us His Word that is described as a sword, "sharper than any double-edged sword" (Heb. 4:12). If you need a sharper instrument with which to craft your arrows, there is none sharper than the Word of God. Make time to study the Bible so that you may pass along the truth, and then trust God with the results. The outcome really is not up to you; the process is.

There are Ten Commandments, but only one comes with a promise. Your child's ability to reap that promise has a lot to do with how that child is parented.

Read Exodus 20:1-17 and write out the promise.

Pray about what you've been learning this week. Ask God to reveal His desires for you and your children. Write them down.

DAY 5
HOW DO I DO IT ALL?

You don't, at least not all at once, because God never intended for us to do it all.

There are moments in a mom's life when God gives you a glimpse of what it's all about—a peek into the profound influence a mom can have on her child's life. During a time in our lives when my family was experiencing stress and strife, I made a conscious decision to daily choose not to carry the stress and strife around in the way I treated my family. Mind you, this is not because I'm some fantastic person. It was because I purposefully spent daily time with God so that I could focus more on Him than on my circumstances. But one night that decision reaped a profound and hopeful moment with my son.

The memory is extremely vivid. My son stood up on his chair at dinnertime, put one arm around my husband's neck and one arm around my neck, looked me and his father in the eyes, and declared very loudly, "I love my life." Those words infused hope into my soul. He had no idea the turmoil brewing, that God had been directing me to press on and remain focused on my family, keeping them a priority while many other important things loomed.

> Trust in the LORD and do good;
> dwell in the land and enjoy safe pasture.
> Take delight in the LORD,
> and he will give you the desires of your heart.
> Commit your way to the LORD;
> trust in him and he will do this:
> He will make your righteous reward shine like the dawn,
> your vindication like the noonday sun.
> **PSALM 37:3-6**

Paraphrase what this verse says to you in your life.

Read Philippians 3:14, and fill in the blanks: "I _____ _____ toward the goal to win the prize for which God has called me heavenward in Christ Jesus."

God does not expect us to have life figured out or to have a perfect track record. Neither does He expect us to do things perfectly. There is peace and hope in doing what God has called you to do as a mom, recognizing the importance of it, and doing what is before you each day.

TAKE ACTION

One of the areas that can make us crazy is dividing our time between all that we must do as moms and all that we want to do as women, based on our gifts and talents.

In matters of time management, let me challenge you to dissect what your motivation is for how you spend each hour of the day. Yes, do what needs to be done to provide for your family, but consider cutting back in areas that are strictly for "self" if your days are getting too harried. This certainly doesn't mean we don't take time to focus on ourselves—which is very important—but it does mean that some things we'd like to do now need to wait.

If God is leading you in this, what's something you could stop doing, for a time, to focus more on your family?

It takes a strong woman to set aside self-interest to put her family first—but strong is exactly what women are!

Thousands of books have been written on time management solutions. But the number one suggestion I have for you in time management is this: Mom, give yourself permission to say no. Anytime you, or one of your kids, are asked to do something new, the first answer should always be, "Let me think and pray about it, and I will get back to you." Then do just that. If you know adding something else won't work, either swap out the new opportunity with something already scheduled or just say no. Really!

List some things you may need to say no to right now.

It may be necessary for you to say no to some opportunities based on what the needs of your family happen to be, but know that those opportunities will not cease; you'll just accept those opportunities when the time is wisest. God often calls us to something far before He wants us to jump in and start doing it. God often plants an idea or passion within us and then uses life to train us for a while before He wants us to take action. We need to patiently and expectantly wait—and, while waiting, be "all in" where He currently has us.

List a few biblical characters who God called but who focused on the tasks at hand while waiting on His timing. I'll give you two examples:

Noah (see Gen. 5:32–10:1)
Mary (Luke 1:29-35; John 19:25-27)

Read Romans 8:25. What does this verse tell you about waiting?

DIG DEEPER

Only you can know best how to manage your time and family, but I do know this to be true: God has given you all that you have personally and within your family for His purposes. More than anything, drown out the noise of what the world is telling you to do to be OK and hear what God is calling you to do. If you seek God and His ways, you'll gain wisdom. Then you must be brave enough to act, in obedience, on His promptings.

God's Word tells us that wisdom is supreme and wisdom comes from God. So dig deep and mine for gold by reading all of Proverbs 3—written by Solomon, a man full of wisdom (see 1 Kings 4:30).

As you read Proverbs 3, write what stands out to you below. Contemplate what God is saying as it relates to you and your family. Then pray that you'll act on those promptings.

GROUP TIME: HOW CAN I FIND ME IN THE MESS?

BEAUTIFUL MESS MOMENT

You may not be there yet, but think it through with me. It's the anticipated moment when your child leaves to go to college or moves out to start a job. Those final years while your child is home can be a tug of war as you figure out the balance between letting go and staying connected. You question whether or not you did all you could to prepare him or her for the challenges ahead.

I hit that same wall when my daughter was preparing to leave for college. I always wanted to be the best mom possible, but I found myself questioning if I had done enough. And who was I without her? She is such a part of me and her life let me live out the dream of being a mom.

☐ *What were your childhood dreams about what you would be when you grew up? How was being a mom part of your dreams?*

DISCUSS

This chapter is titled "How Can I Find Me in the Mess?" which really makes me laugh because I think of myself as the mess—not just a part of it! I'm far from perfect, and if you listen to my children, sometimes weird. In my mess, I'm a mom, but I'm much more than a mom. But sometimes it's difficult for my children or others to understand and grasp when they only see the mom part of me.

☐ *What about you? Are you lost in the beautiful mess that is your life? What are some of the things that you think define who you are and your place in life?*

Sometimes the way we see ourselves is distinctly different from the way others view us. Take time in your group to let others share and encourage one another on the positive qualities and characteristics they observe in one another.

As a group, dive into Proverbs 31:10-31 and answer the following questions.

☐ What are the positives about this woman as she relates to her husband?

☐ What is her work ethic?

☐ How would you describe her attitude and actions toward her community?

☐ How does she treat her home and family?

Does she seem too perfect to you? Are you thinking, *How will I ever live up to that?* We'll get into this more this week, but Proverbs 31 is meant to be less of a comparison and more of a call. Look at Proverbs 31:25-31 again with your group.

☐ What are some of this woman's secrets? What stands out most to you?

☐ Where do you think she finds her strength, honor, and the ability to laugh at an unknown future? Where does she find wisdom to give loving instruction to others?

☐ It says that she "fears the LORD" (v. 30). What does that mean to you?

☐ Consider the following. What if finding you in the middle of the beautiful mess that is your life means discovering and being all God created you to be? What if being a mom is only a part of that? What do you feel is missing?

WEEK 5

HOW CAN I FIND ME IN THE MESS?

For many years, I've had the secret thought that if the Proverbs 31 woman shops at the Piggly Wiggly, I hope she doesn't get behind me in the checkout line. I'm the woman who has to hunt and dig for her store loyalty card. You know, the card that has a handy pre-punched hole so it can be attached to my keychain? But of course I always fling it back in my purse so it can sink to the bottom to rest between the one-eyed sunglasses and the three inkless ball-point pens. Then I have to rifle through my wallet for my debit card. It's usually at that moment when I remember it's sitting at home on the counter, where I used it to pry open the pickle jar.

At any moment my purse could supply random items like a car-wash receipt or that static-y sock I found stuck to the inside of my pants leg at church. You never know when you might be called upon to play a junk-in-your-purse scavenger hunt. Just call me Miss Prepared.

In truth, I rarely feel prepared. But what I do feel is lacking when I compare myself to passages like Proverbs 31. The Proverbs 31 woman's children rise up and call her blessed. Her husband sings her praises. She's organized and fearless and creative—all the things I want to be but often think I'm not.

It hasn't been until recent years that I've realized that Proverbs 31 is less of a comparison chart and more of a call—a call to fall into the arms of a God who dreams big for me and who has special plans just for me. It's a call to believe in myself like the God who made me does.

As we dig into some of the aspects of Proverbs 31 and other verses, let your mind drop any preconceived notion of what the perfect woman might look like or be. Instead, let God take you on a trip where you dream together of what you might become hand in hand with Him. You've already captivated His heart; now let His delight sink into your soul.

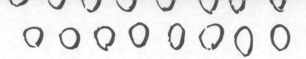

DAY 1
FAR FROM PERFECT

Her children arise and call her blessed;
her husband also, and he praises her.
PROVERBS 31:28

When my daughter was in middle school, I (Sherry) loved being able to pick her up from school. Sometimes we'd stop at Sonic for a cold drink, and I always enjoyed hearing about her day and the funny things that had happened in the classroom. But I remember a particular day that was not so joyful. On the way home, she reminded me that I had forgotten to pack the sandwich she had requested and asked where the dollar was that she had told me three times she needed for milk.

As we pulled into the driveway, I reminded her it was her turn to get the garbage cans from the end of the driveway. She slid out, slammed the door in a huff, and marched down to where the driveway met the street. In a few minutes she came marching back. "Mom, come with me!" I followed her back down the driveway and without a word, she pointed at the ground.

I could feel the horror creep up my neck and into my cheeks. The night before, I had lugged the trash cans down the drive for the trash men to pick up, into which I had deposited a big plastic bag stuffed with old underwear after some spring cleaning. Now staring at me were two pair of my raggedy, worn-out undies. They had lain there all day. For the whole world to see.

I tried to explain to my daughter that I had tied the bag tight and put the lid on securely. The trash men must've ripped the bag as they threw it on the truck. She didn't want to hear it. I distinctly heard her mutter as she marched back up the driveway, "Now we're going to have to move!"

On that day, I'm positive the last thing my daughter wanted to do was to rise up and call me blessed.

Have you ever felt this way? Like you're the number one enemy of your children? I've come to realize this is part of being a mom. While it's not my goal to embarrass the life out of my kids, it's important that they see the imperfection that is me. It's even more important that they see I'm able to laugh and not take myself so seriously. I see this too in the Proverbs 31 woman.

She is clothed with strength and dignity;
she can laugh at the days to come.
PROVERBS 31:25

What in the world could be dignified about leaving your unmentionables at the end of the driveway, you might ask? Actually nothing. But I can model strength and dignity in my response to the imperfection that is me. I mess up. I make mistakes. But I can admit them and realize they won't kill me. I can even laugh at them. How great for my kids to see! And this is what matters most.

We're going to fail as moms and wives and daughters. It's inevitable that we will disappoint the people we care the most about in our lives. But we are each the Proverbs 31 woman when we respond with grace and humility and are able to do our best and not take ourselves too seriously.

Spend a few minutes reading Proverbs 31:10-31, and let's see what we can learn.

> A wife of noble character who can find? She is worth far more than rubies. Her husband has full confidence in her and lacks nothing of value. She brings him good, not harm, all the days of her life. She selects wool and flax and works with eager hands. She is like the merchant ships, bringing her food from afar. She gets up while it is still night; she provides food for her family and portions for her female servants. She considers a field and buys it; out of her earnings she plants a vineyard. She sets about her work vigorously; her arms are strong for her tasks. She sees that her trading is profitable, and her lamp does not go out at night. In her hand she holds the distaff and grasps the spindle with her fingers. She opens her arms to the poor and extends her hands to the needy. When it snows, she has no fear for her household; for all of them are clothed in scarlet. She makes coverings for her bed; she is clothed in fine linen and purple. Her husband is respected at the city gate, where he takes his seat among the elders of the land. She makes linen garments and sells them, and supplies the merchants with sashes. She is clothed with strength and dignity; she can laugh at the days to come. She speaks with wisdom, and faithful instruction is on her tongue. She watches over the affairs of her household and does not eat the bread of idleness. Her children arise and call her blessed; her husband also, and he praises her: "Many women do noble things, but

you surpass them all." Charm is deceptive, and beauty is fleeting; but a woman who fears the LORD is to be praised. Honor her for all that her hands have done, and let her works bring her praise at the city gate.
PROVERBS 31:10-31

Whew, this is quite a list isn't it? When I read the Proverbs 31 list, I automatically tick off the things I'm OK at and the areas where I think I fall short. This woman is talented and ever-busy. Her eyes are turned to the needs of others. She makes her husband and children proud—something I don't always see in myself so I tend to use this part of the passage as a self-condemnation, especially when my family is irritated at me. But I don't think this is what God had in mind at all.

In fact, some commentaries indicate that this passage isn't even describing a real woman, but that it is a mom's letter to her son, describing the things to look for in a future wife. Instead of a "shame on you for what you are not," God is calling us to be the best we can be. He isn't calling us to compare ourselves to an impossible standard that discourages us. Instead, He is calling us to hold His hand while we pursue our best selves through His power and might.

What attributes of the Proverbs 31 woman jump out at you? Are they things you're good at doing or things you think you could never be?

Are there things about you that you wish weren't a part of you? If so, what are they? Where do these feelings originate?

How do you model the ability to laugh at yourself for your children?

TAKE ACTION

Read verse 30 again:

> Charm is deceptive and beauty is fleeting,
> but a woman who fears the LORD will be praised.

The most essential part of the Proverbs 31 woman is her relationship with the Lord. This verse reminds us that what's on the outside won't last, and what others think ultimately doesn't matter. God is looking for us to serve Him with whole hearts and to realize it's His power—not our own—that's at work in our lives. He already loves us and wants us to be faithful daughters who love and worship Him. When we focus solely on God and His will for our lives, He will give us the wisdom we need, no matter what parenthood may bring our way. Like the Proverbs 31 woman, we can accomplish so much for God when we intentionally choose to draw our strength from Him.

How do you handle worry as a mom?

How do you enable yourself to be carefree in the midst of pressure, anxiety, failure, or criticism? How can you share this with your children?

How can recognizing God's power over your life in the small things help you face difficulties with confidence instead of worry or anxiety?

DIG DEEPER

Sometimes the Proverbs 31 passage can feel a bit like finger wagging and "this is what you should be." When we read the exhaustive list, we feel like we just can't measure up. The Word of God isn't meant to paralyze us, but to set us free to be the women of God we're uniquely called to be.

How can you find freedom in your uniqueness based on Proverbs 31?

DAY 2
OWNING YOUR OWN UNIQUENESS

Her name was Dina, and when she spoke, she stuttered. The first time we had a conversation, it was hard for me not to jump in and finish her sentences for her. I found myself feeling sorry for her. Her speech seemed so halting. But soon I realized Dina didn't feel sorry for herself. She was confident and self-assured. She had a tangible peace about her that drew you in.

After we had known each other for several months, we had a conversation about her stuttering. She said that as a child, it was something she'd hated. It embarrassed her. She loved to talk to people and, in her head, the ideas all lined up nicely. But when they came out of her mouth, they seemed to get stuck. As a teenager, she was so embarrassed that many times she avoided social situations.

Dina said that as she got older, she realized it was a gift in disguise. She had learned in her silence to listen. Really listen. And as she did, she noticed that listening was a skill that many people didn't have. They were too busy talking. But she had gotten really good at listening to the words and considering what the other person was thinking and feeling. She said that listening gave her a chance not only to choose her responses carefully, but also to take time to pray for the person she was listening to.

Isn't it compelling when someone is able to embrace something difficult about herself and use it to her advantage?

Dina is a living illustration of Psalm 139:14—"I am fearfully and wonderfully made." We are each different. Different doesn't have to be odd or strange. It can be beautiful and wonderful. Getting to know Dina made me truly feel like I had been in the presence of a beautifully and wonderfully made individual.

Dina had become comfortable with what was different about herself and had realized that she was made on purpose with a unique purpose to fulfill.

How about you? What is unique about you?

Maybe it's something about your appearance (like red hair) that you feel sets you apart in a good way. Or maybe it's something you don't like—such as wide hips, crooked teeth, or the way you talk.

What things make you unique as a mom?

While Moses clearly wasn't a mom, he was a leader, and he struggled with things that were unique about him. Exodus gives us a glimpse of this as Moses complained about his slowness of speech and tongue.

> Moses said to the LORD, "Pardon your servant, Lord. I have never been eloquent, neither in the past nor since you have spoken to your servant. I am slow of speech and tongue."
> **EXODUS 4:10**

Some scholars believe Moses had a speech impediment, perhaps a stutter. And it's clear that Moses felt like his speech prohibited him from being an effective communicator. However, God didn't see it that way.

When God called Moses to be the one to speak on behalf of the enslaved Israelites, Moses told Him he wasn't the right one over and over and over. The Lord responded to Moses this way:

> The LORD said to him, "Who gave human beings their mouths? Who makes them deaf or mute? Who gives them sight or makes them blind? Is it not I, the LORD? Now go; I will help you speak and will teach you what to say."
> **EXODUS 4:11-12**

Moses was so caught up in his fears that he was missing the invitation God extended to him to be His voice and to bring justice to His people. Moses missed how the Lord had created him, with unique skills and gifts to perform this important task.

TAKE ACTION

Have you ever felt like you lacked ability or skill as a mom and it held you back?

Like Moses, have you ever said, "Excuse me, God, surely You must be mistaken. Susie is a much better person to serve You"?

Psalm 139 is a great chapter to read and rest in to absorb how God has uniquely created *you* for each season of life He has given you. God knows your weaknesses and your strengths. He knows when you will fail, and He knows your greatest victories. He weeps with you, and He rejoices with you. He created you to be beautiful, wonderful, and messy you!

> Your eyes saw my unformed body;
> all the days ordained for me were written in your book
> before one of them came to be.
> **PSALM 139:16**

Read Psalm 139:1-24.

What might God want to say to you through these verses?

What do you believe God "knit" into you from birth?

Do you see purpose in it that relates to being a mom, a wife, a friend, or a daughter?

What is He developing in you now?

Can you articulate to someone else the ways that you are "fearfully and wonderfully made"? Is it uncomfortable for you to do this? Why or why not?

Read this verse again.

> See if there is any offensive way in me,
> and lead me in the way everlasting.
> **PSALM 139:24**

What might God want to work on in your life?

DIG DEEPER

Is there something about yourself that you have had a hard time reconciling? Is it something about your physical appearance or circumstances or personality?

Consider sharing this thing with a trusted friend who loves you. Tell her how you feel about it. Share how you view it in yourself—how you feel it is hard to deal with or how it holds you back. Then ask yourself and your friend, *How could I use this for good?* Consider the answer. *Do I feel like it fits into the parameters of being fearfully and wonderfully made?* Think about the ways God could use it to help someone else or a way you could use it to grow.

DAY 3
I'M MORE THAN A MOM.

Each of you should use whatever gift you have received to serve others, as faithful stewards of God's grace in its various forms.
1 PETER 4:10

I knew the day would come, and it was here. My firstborn was graduating from high school. I looked at him in his graduation cap and gown, and I felt like my heart might burst open and send forth a never-ending gush of pride. He was so smart and so handsome. I suppressed the urge to scream out, "That's *my* baby!" when his name was called to cross the platform. My son never realized how close he had come to being humiliated.

When my husband and I dropped him off at college, I couldn't stop the tears. He looked grown up and so young all at the same time. *Would he get enough to eat? What if he was lonely? What kind of people was he going to come in contact with?* The questions swirled in my head like a building tornado.

We helped him settle in his room, and as I wrapped my arms around his man shoulders to say good-bye, I felt again like my heart was going to burst. This time, though, the pressure was different, full of mom uncertainty. *What would it mean to parent this man-child now that he was out on his own? Would he still need me?* He was about to launch into a life that wouldn't intersect with mine. *What did it all mean?*

Looking back on that day, I realize now I didn't need to be so panicky. Yes, he most certainly found his way to the cafeteria and found enough food to eat. Yes, he bumped up against some very different people, but it helped him refine his worldview and make decisions on what he really believed. He still came home from time to time with his bursting bag of smelly laundry and an empty gas tank. I was still a mom, though it looked a little different.

Have you wondered what mom life will be like after your child moves out? Maybe you are already there. If you are like me, it raised some pretty important questions. *What comes next? Who did God design me to be in addition to being a mom? Now that I have a little more time, a little more brain space, and a little more freedom, what will I become?*

The story of the mom in Proverbs 31 can shed some light on these questions. God's plan is big and far reaching, for every one of us. Verses 13-20 shed some light on her activity.

She selects wool and flax
and works with eager hands.
She is like the merchant ships,
bringing her food from afar.
She gets up while it is still night;
she provides food for her family
and portions for her female servants.
She considers a field and buys it;
out of her earnings she plants a vineyard.
She sets about her work vigorously;
her arms are strong for her tasks.
She sees that her trading is profitable,
and her lamp does not go out at night.
In her hand she holds the distaff
and grasps the spindle with her fingers.
She opens her arms to the poor
and extends her hands to the needy.
PROVERBS 31:13-20

Whew, this is one busy momma! Take note that this woman uses her talents all over the place. She's a business woman and she applies her ingenuity and creativity to bless her family.

Also note that she's busy outside of her house, using her gifts and talents to bless others. She makes sure her family is cared for and takes pride in it, but also knows that her skills can make a difference in her community. We don't know how old this woman's children are, but we get the picture that when her children are grown, she won't be sitting and thinking, *Hmm, I wonder what God has for me?* She's already using her gifts beyond her family.

What do verses 13-20 mean to you as a mom?

It says loud and clear that your job as a mom is critically important. What you do every day matters. You meet the needs of your children and husband, and you bless them. And as big as this task is, this passage also reminds us as moms that He designed us with passions and giftings beyond being a mom.

I'm always sad when I hear a mom say, "I'm just a mom." There really is no "just" about it. Being a mom is a very big thing, but it's not the only thing. You are a mom—and you are a woman, a daughter, and a friend. You may also be a wife, a volunteer, an employee, or a business owner. And these are all good and godly things. What I take away from the Proverbs 31 passage is a gentle reminder to develop myself in all the areas that God has gifted me—and not to wait until my children are grown up and out of the house to do it.

How are you developing this in yourself?

Is there something you're passionate about but haven't gotten involved in yet? If so, what do you think might be holding you back? If you're pursuing a passion outside of your family, has it helped you be a better woman or friend or mom? How?

Research shows that being a well-rounded woman who develops her passions and skills helps her children learn to be well-rounded as well. Have you seen this at work in your family? How?

Do you struggle with finding passions or things to focus on outside of being a mom? If so, what's one area you would like to explore for learning or volunteer opportunities? To help you identify a place to start, think about gifts and talents that others have recognized in you.

What did you love to do before your first child was born that you don't do anymore? Do you see busyness crowding out things that you used to do that brought you joy?

How do you let your children see you develop yourself outside of being a mom? What impact does it have on your children?

If nothing were impossible and you had the resources, what would you accomplish for God?

TAKE ACTION

One of the most important ways to discover who we are in Christ is to help others outside of our own family. Where can you make a difference in the lives of others? Is there a volunteer opportunity in your church? Could you and a few friends begin a group for other young moms in your neighborhood? Is there a community program you could volunteer in? Make a specific plan to contribute to someone else's life in the next month.

DIG DEEPER

Set an hour this week to reflect on what your ideal day would look like. Write a description of it in a journal. Questions to consider include:

How do you connect with God during the day?
How do your children spend their day?
What new things are you learning?
What volunteer service do you perform?
Are you involved in marketplace activity? If so, what are you doing?
If you're married, how do you spend time with your husband?
How are you connecting with friends? With your extended family?

If you described your ideal day, reflect on these questions:

What parts of your description can you begin praying about?
What things can you act on today?
What can you talk with your spouse or friends about?

AM I PAYING ATTENTION TO ME?

Cast all your anxiety on him because he cares for you. Be
alert and of sober mind. Your enemy the devil prowls around
like a roaring lion looking for someone to devour.
1 PETER 5:7-8

"Are you paying attention to Sherry?" This was a question from my mentor to which I replied, "Sherry who?" My friend gave me a hard look. She meant me, of course, but I didn't understand what my mentor was asking. *Had I forgotten to get completely dressed? Was something hanging out that shouldn't be? Did I have spinach in my teeth?* She explained she wasn't talking about my appearance. She was talking about what was on the inside, what was going on in my heart and in my emotions. Was I taking care of me so I could take care of others?

Great question, because we don't always do this.

Moms cook and clean and do for others, often forgetting to do anything for themselves. A young mom named Sara shared this story with me.

> I don't like Tuesdays. It's the day Jim, my husband, has to work late, and I have the kids all day by myself. Last Tuesday, I got up and immediately had to feed the baby. Then I attacked the mountain of laundry and tried to find out what was causing the bad smell in the refrigerator. While I was cleaning, I realized that my 2-year-old had crawled in the pantry and dumped a whole pound of sugar on the floor. By the time I found her, she had eaten quite a bit of it, and the floor was a gritty, sticky mess. It wasn't long before the diarrhea started, and I got to spend even more time in the laundry room. By six o'clock I realized I hadn't eaten anything all day, and I felt so tired and crabby that I snapped at Jim when he walked in the door, complaining about the smell that was still coming from the refrigerator. I couldn't wait for that Tuesday to end!

Sara is not alone. Many moms tend to all the tasks of the day—whether at the office or at home—forgetting to tend to the critical parts of themselves. And when she does, she puts herself at risk.

Read again from 1 Peter:

> Your enemy the devil prowls around like a roaring
> lion looking for someone to devour.
> **1 PETER 5:8**

As moms, we have a very real enemy, and it's not our 2-year-old eating sugar in the pantry, or our husband who may or may not be doing his fair share. It's Satan. He wants you to be exhausted and overwhelmed. He wants to discourage you with circumstances. He wants to find you tired and weak so he can attack. The way to combat this is to pay attention to your mom heart and invest in the areas that feed you. In partnership with Barna Research, MOPS International has developed five critical attributes that a mom can invest in to help her be her healthy best.

1. **HER EMOTIONAL CORE.** As a mom you need to feed your emotional self with moments away from your children, free from worry and anxiety. Do you take opportunities to relax and do something that brings you joy, such as reading a favorite book or exercising? When you notice your shoulders getting tight and your voice sounding snappish, do you have a strategy to relax and unwind? Every mom needs an outlet for creativity and relaxation, one that gets her back in touch with who she is as a woman, a wife, and friend.

2. **HER CIRCLE OF SUPPORT.** Moms not only needs friends to laugh with, but they also need parenting support in the form of a mentor or parent that they can talk to.

3. **HER SPIRITUAL DEVELOPMENT.** This is central to your emotional resilience and how you view your role as a mom. Being plugged into a life-giving church and a small group are vitally helpful.

4. **HER MARRIAGE.** Our research showed that for married moms, having a good relationship with her husband was central to how she felt she was doing as a mom. For unmarried moms, having another key support person or partner is essential in her core development as a mom.

5. **HER MOM FINESSE.** Every mom needs development in practical parenting skills to build her self-esteem and mom confidence. From our research, this could come from books and seminars, but most practically came from mentor learning and connections with other moms.

Moms know that they need proper rest and nutrition to function well, but paying attention to yourself goes deeper than that. God has an incredible plan for your life, and He didn't design you to travel the mom road alone—without leaning on the support opportunities He designed to be part of our lives. Take a minute to do a self-assessment in the five critical areas mentioned above.

How are you doing with paying attention to you?

How strong is your emotional resilience? Do you have a hard time managing your emotions on a daily basis? Or do you bounce back pretty quickly after a disappointment or emotional event on a daily basis? How do you feel about your answer?

Do you have a circle of friends who help you relax and have fun? Can you name a specific mom friend who makes you smile and that you can learn from? Do you have a mom mentor or friend you can lean on for prayer or advice?

Are you part of a life-giving church body? Do you worship regularly? Do you spend time in God's Word? Do you have a regular spiritual rhythm that helps you grow?

If you're married, how is your relationship with your husband? Do you feel your marriage is a support to your role as a mom? Are you actively communicating with your husband how you can support each other?

If you're not married, do you have a support partner whom you can trust and lean on? If not, brainstorm who that person could be.

Are you working on your parenting skills? Is there a particular parenting skill you'd like to grow in? How can you grow that skill?

TAKE ACTION

Pick one critical area mentioned above that you would like to grow in. Find a mom friend to talk over your thoughts and to help you develop an action plan. For your action plan, think about ways you could rearrange your schedule to make room for new ideas and people you could talk with to help you implement your ideas.

DIG DEEPER

On a sheet of paper or in your journal, create a personal timeline that marks your history. Document your events, giving the date of the event, explaining the event in one or two sentences, and drawing or adding a picture. As you do this, remember that no event is too small for your timeline. What matters is that it was significant to you.

Looking at your timeline, journal about how each event changed and shaped you. Take time to pray over the past God has given you, give Him your present, and trust Him with your future.

Don't feel like you need to accomplish a project of this nature in one day. This is a longer-term project that allows you to consider your own life and your story going forward. Take time to listen to God and what He might be saying to you through the life circumstances He has allowed you to experience.

DAY 5

WHAT DOES GOD SAY ABOUT ME?

My friend and colleague Anne is a working mother of two preschoolers. Her days start early, as she wrestles children into clothes and debates their breakfast choices. ("No, you may not eat a cupcake for breakfast.") All the while, she's trying to get herself present-able for work. Some days the drop off at school goes like a dream, and other days, she gets to work in tears over an already long day—and it's only 9:00 a.m.

After a busy day at work, she gets home around 6:00 p.m. and tries to get her children fed, bathed, and in bed at a reasonable hour. She says she tries hard to laugh and be lighthearted, but sometimes she doesn't succeed when she thinks ahead to the house-work she'll have to tackle before she can go to bed herself.

Anne loves her work—both as a mom and in her job—but some days she just doesn't feel like she is winning. Is anyone getting her best? Some days she's just not sure. She is confident she is right where God wants her to be, but the long days and fleeting time leave Anne weary and wondering how the Proverbs 31 woman survived.

Have you ever felt weariness as a mother, questioning whether what you're doing is best for your children, or even if you're enough for them?

As a mom, in whatever season of life you find yourself in, I want you to know deep in your soul that God delights in *you*—no matter how you see yourself. Do you ever think, *Sure, maybe God likes me or puts up with me. After all, He is God.* When you picture God delighting in you—especially when you look in the mirror and see a tired face and the mess around you that needs your attention—it's sometimes hard to believe. Yet read the following verse:

> The LORD your God is with you,
> the Mighty Warrior who saves.
> He will take great delight in you;
> in his love he will no longer rebuke you,
> but will rejoice over you with singing.
> **ZEPHANIAH 3:17**

This verse doesn't say, "God will delight in you when you get it all together." In fact, it doesn't have any qualifiers. It just says you delight Him. You—just as you are, imperfect and wonderful—delight the heart of God. Let's marinate in this verse for a minute.

Take a moment to consider your children and how they delight you. Maybe it's his sweet baby toes or her lopsided smile or his endless knock-knock jokes. Maybe it's the beauty of her face or his big, almost-man shoulders. It's different things for everyone, but whatever it is, when you see it in your children, your heart lights up. Doesn't it just fill you with joy to picture the best and beautiful about your children?

I have two granddaughters, Maggie Claire and Mollie Rose, who make messes and at times are noisy and demanding. The other night, I came home from work and gave Mollie Rose, who just had her first birthday, a cookie. She sucked and smacked on it, turning it into a mushy mess. Then she promptly stuck it in my leather boot—while I was still wearing it. In the moment, this didn't bring a smile to my face. In fact, it made me feel a little bit grumpy. But there's nothing that little girl could ever do to make me love her one bit less.

I know you feel the same way about your children. Despite their imperfections, your love for them knows no walls. It has no end, and you delight in them. This is the kind of crazy, never ending, no-matter-what kind of love that Zephaniah is talking about. Your children do nothing to earn your delight; they simply are yours. You don't expect perfection from your kids, and God feels the exact same way about you.

> Repeat the sentence to yourself: "God delights in me no matter how I view myself." Write it on a card that you can pull out on the days you feel discouraged. Post it on your mirror so you see it first thing in the morning. Read it. Say it out loud. Rest in the fact that this verse is true, and it was written for you.

TAKE ACTION

Perhaps you're thinking how it's easier said than done to rest in God's delight over you. Consider these questions in understanding the delight of God in you.

> What do you think of when you see yourself in the mirror? What words come to mind?

Now picture God standing right beside you in front of the mirror. What words do you think He would use? Write them down. Do they match up with Zephaniah 3:17?

If every mom could walk in the confidence that God delights in them, how do you think it would affect our world?

If you struggle living day-to-day in the delight that God feels for you, where do you think this struggle comes from? Does it come from others, from your circumstances, or from the voice inside your head?

Do your children believe that God delights in them? How can you model what living in this looks like?

DIG DEEPER

Ponder the things about you that make God smile. Consider all the good things about you, including the talent He has given you, how you use your personality and compassion to help others, what you do to care for your family, and how you worship Him with what He has blessed you with.

List the ways you think God delights in you. Write out every positive attribute that you can think of and don't hold back!

Now thank God for everything on the list! Thank Him for making you this way. Ask Him how He can continue to grow the good parts of you, and how you can use those things to honor Him.

Spend some time reading over Zephaniah 3:17 again, using it as a prayer. Ask the Lord to show you how He rejoices over you. Come back to your list and add anything you feel God is telling you from your time of prayer. Review the list when you're feeling discouraged. Take a deep breath and rest in the knowledge that you are more than enough.

GROUP TIME: WHAT DOES GOD WANT TO SAY TO ME?

BEAUTIFUL MESS MOMENT

It was one of those cute preschool programs to mark the end of the year. The 4- and 5-year-olds heading off to kindergarten the next fall stood tall and proud with their posterboard-created graduation caps as the teacher read where they planned to attend elementary school and the career path they were currently pursuing. Fireman. Policeman. Spider-man. They were adorable. But the one who touched me the most was the girl who said "Mommy." There were several who valued the role of mothers, even at such a young age. Of all the things they could see themselves doing in the future, motherhood rose to the top.

How do you beat yourself up and focus on your mistakes and failures more than on your successes?

DISCUSS
Think back on your mom or others who fulfilled the mom role in your life. What did you admire about her? What did you want to emulate when you became a mom?

As we admire and look up to other moms, what are some of the unrealistic expectations we put on ourselves?

Face it moms. We may want to be Superwoman, but our children just want Mommy. What do you think children need most from their mothers?

What do you think God wants to say to you about your role as the mom of your children?

Read Ephesians 2:10. God is preparing you for the different stages and seasons of motherhood. It may not always look like it or feel like it, but He is. Think about the different ways your role as mom has or will change in each of the following seasons. Look at the examples and write down your responses to discuss with your group.

Preschool (birth to 5) Protector	Elementary (ages 5 to 10) Teacher	Preteen (ages 10 to 13) Counselor	Teen (ages 13 to18) Supervisor	Adult (age 18 and up) Advisor

Being a mom is challenging. It's a fine balance to shift from one season to the next. As moms, we learn as much as our children do while continuing to pour into them, yet while still allowing them independence and responsibility. It can be some of the most difficult days as we teach our children to own their failures and take responsibility for their mistakes.

- ☐ *How have you seen a concerned mom protect and hover too much over her child? How did her actions hinder her son or daughter?*

- ☐ *How have you seen a mom give her children too much freedom? How did her actions hinder her son or daughter?*

- ☐ *What seasons of motherhood are you most concerned about or afraid to face? Why?*

- ☐ *As you complete this final week of Beautiful Mess, what do you think God wants to say to you most? How will your life be different because of what God is teaching you?*

WEEK 6

WHAT DOES GOD WANT
TO SAY TO ME?

We've come a long way together in exploring our beautiful mess! Motherhood truly is a miracle, and Jesus' first miracle is where we will end our journey together in this final week.

The day started out like most days had over the previous 18 years, and that wasn't a bad thing. Our home life is lighthearted, filled with activity and laughter. I'm known as a "fun" mom—a title I really like—and the relationships I have with my two teenaged children are close. Our family has moved four times since the children were young, so we've learned to depend on each other. We're tight.

On this particular day, even the weather seemed to be on our side. Spring had come. But what I didn't know was that something was stirring (festering may be a better word) inside me, and within hours it would spill out of me and all over my unsuspecting kids.

When they arrived home from school, I was in the kitchen, preparing dinner. They unwound a bit, and then started working on their chores. Theoretically. We crossed paths several times and, in my observation, not a whole lot of work was actually getting done. Even my exhortation, "Hey, let's hurry up and finish so we can have a good night when Dad gets home," was ignored—tossed aside as a mere suggestion.

My children know I don't like confrontation; it messes with my joyful and energetic outlook. Confrontation drains me. So when faced with a lack of cooperation, I generally use friendly, challenging banter to motivate. Occasionally I'll really dial it up and threaten "No fun for you this weekend!"

However, on this day I had a different reaction. And I must confess, as it turns out, it was more than just the emotional buildup of this one day. A series of days, months, and years had snuck up on me. Unspoken hurts have a tendency to do that.

Join me in day 1 of this week for the rest of the story.

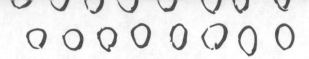

THE MOMENT … CONTINUES.

It was the spring of my daughter's senior year of high school, and thoughts of all I (Tracey) had not yet done to prepare her had been troubling me. For several days I had been privately beating myself up for some poor mothering choices, replaying in my mind mistakes I'd made and opportunities I'd missed. I agonized over my personality flaws and shortcomings, especially those that had manifested in my children. I recognized that these flaws could turn into major issues in their lives, and I surmised it would all be my fault. I was mired in a thick sludge of regret, feeling inadequate as a mother.

Then my pensiveness took a little turn and my instinct for self-preservation took over. As I reviewed the years of being a dedicated mother, I came up with a mental list of all the things I had done right—all the sacrifice, the hours spent with my children, the life of intentionality, the fun times of a thriving home. I'd actually done a pretty good job.

There was a battle raging within me: bad mother vs. good mother.

I had been spinning all of this in my mind for who knows how long, but in the span of mere moments, while hearing my teenagers laugh and carry on down the hallway, I suddenly came to the conclusion that all I had done for them over the years didn't matter to them. I asked them join me at the kitchen table. As I looked into the big brown eyes of my beautiful daughter, Samara, and the soft green eyes of my handsome son, Westley, I saw before me the children I so desperately loved and wanted to launch well. And I was slammed with the reality that they were slipping away. She was soon to leave for college, and life would never be the same. He was more than six feet tall, more man than boy, and had been pulling away from me and toward his father.

I felt I didn't matter anymore.

I started to cry. Through my tears, I saw wide eyes, filled with compassion and confusion. Then I heard, "What's wrong, Mom?" My reply would prove prophetic: "All I do is pour the water." Of course they didn't understand what I meant and they were waiting for an explanation.

Before either of them was born, I was the membership director at a country club. The wait staff in the restaurant used to talk about how all the rich people ignored them and didn't even see them when they were dining. It bothered me that people saw the staff as so unimportant, and I used to think that the club members believed, "All they do is pour the water." The diners always had a full glass. They expected it but never cared to notice who filled it up.

I said to my children, "Sometimes in our home I feel like all I ever do is pour the water. No one notices . . . or cares." More weeping.

I remember looking up and seeing them staring at each other. I could see that they were processing this together, and somehow that mattered. The unspoken bond between siblings who love each other comforted me. But something more was happening. I think my children began to see me in a different light, realizing that I had self-doubt, that I carried around my own issues, that I had weaknesses and frailties.

I've always tried to teach my children to have hearts of gratitude. What we learned in that moment is though they express gratitude to others, lately they had been failing to express gratitude to me or their dad. And with all the family changes going on in our home, they needed to be mindful that it was affecting all of us. We ended up having a great discussion on the importance of showing gratitude to me and their dad, reinforcing the training of how to treat their roommates in college and even their future spouses.

Though the conversation started through tears, it ended with laughter and hugs. They promised to work to do better at showing gratitude, and I gave an apology for laying my issues on them.

Yet, even with all this progress, the real lesson of the moment wasn't clear to me until the next morning. (We'll explore that lesson together in day 2.)

TAKE ACTION

Share a time in your own mom life when you've felt like no one noticed you or cared about you. With a heart to understand how God might use that time, write it down and unburden yourself.

[1]LORD, our Lord,
how majestic is your name in all the earth!
You have set your glory
in the heavens.
[2]Through the praise of children and infants
you have established a stronghold against your enemies,
to silence the foe and the avenger.
[3]When I consider your heavens,
the work of your fingers,
the moon and the stars,
which you have set in place,
[4]what is mankind that you are mindful of them,
human beings that you care for them?
[5]You have made them a little lower than the angels
and crowned them with glory and honor.
[6]You made them rulers over the works of your hands;
you put everything under their feet:
[7]all flocks and herds,
and the animals of the wild,
[8]the birds in the sky,
and the fish in the sea,
all that swim the paths of the seas.
[9]LORD, our Lord,
how majestic is your name in all the earth!
PSALM 8

Spend some time contemplating who God is, how vast He is, and how He is totally and completely mindful of you (see v. 4).

How does it make you feel that God sees you and cares about you?

Verses 6-8 point out all that humankind is in charge of and called to care for. List what God has put you in charge of and what He has called you to care for as a mom.

Our ability to grow in our knowledge of God and His ways is a God-given gift. We can live a fulfilling life—even one that's a beautiful mess—when we know we're following a divine calling.

Read 2 Peter 1:3-4 and pray that verse over you and your family.

DIG DEEPER

Jesus so completely loves us—regardless of who we are, what we've done, or what we haven't done. Seeking a relationship with Him by spending time praying and reading God's Word truly does provide peace and enables a joyful perspective.

If you're feeling tired and burdened, decide right now to spend time with God, learning what He can do for you—if only you will let Him.

> [28]"Come to me, all you who are weary and burdened, and I will give you rest. [29]Take my yoke upon you and learn from me, for I am gentle and humble in heart, and you will find rest for your souls. [30]For my yoke is easy and my burden is light."
> MATTHEW 11:28-30

What does Jesus want to give you (see v. 28)?

What does Jesus say you will find for your soul (see v. 29)?

How are the things we each carry for Jesus described (see v. 30)?

In this passage, Jesus explains that He will free you from your heavy load and give you rest. A relationship with Him turns your weary load into purpose and God-inspired intentional living. You begin to know the difference between what you're needlessly carrying and what He intends to carry with you for His divine purposes.

Pray that God will reveal that to you. Then write down what He brings to mind.

JESUS' FIRST MIRACLE = MOM PERSPECTIVE

Strict routines are not my thing. I'm more inclined to the unpremeditated approach, much to my husband's chagrin. Still, most mornings begin in the kitchen as a family before everyone heads out for the day. Then, at random points during the day, I fit in a quiet time, working, cleaning, exercising, and other items on my to-do list. Being random seems to allow more room for interruptions, and something one learns with age is that interruptions are often God's method for teaching deeper truths. Fighting the interruptions often causes us to sidestep the lessons and the blessings.

If Moses had ignored the burning bush atop the mountain because that route wasn't in his plan, he might have missed a divine appointment (see Ex. 3). If David had avoided Goliath because he was just too scared to fight, he might have jeopardized his future as a warrior king (see 1 Sam. 17). If Ruth had not remained loyal to Naomi because she couldn't see past her own grief, she might have never met Boaz (see Ruth 1–4).

God interrupts for good cause. Sometimes He shouts, and sometimes He whispers. This time was more of a whisper when, after finishing my daily reading the morning after the gratitude conversation with my kids, I felt prompted to open my Bible again and read a familiar passage in John 2.

> On the third day a wedding took place at Cana in Galilee.
> Jesus' mother was there, and Jesus and his disciples had
> also been invited to the wedding. When the wine was gone,
> Jesus' mother said to him, "They have no more wine."
> "Woman, why do you involve me?" Jesus
> replied. "My hour has not yet come."
> His mother said to the servants, "Do whatever he tells you."
> Nearby stood six stone water jars, the kind used by the Jews for
> ceremonial washing, each holding from twenty to thirty gallons.
> Jesus said to the servants, "Fill the jars with
> water"; so they filled them to the brim.
> Then he told them, "Now draw some out and
> take it to the master of the banquet."
> They did so, and the master of the banquet tasted the water that
> had been turned into wine. He did not realize where it had come

from, though the servants who had drawn the water knew. Then he called the bridegroom aside and said, "Everyone brings out the choice wine first and then the cheaper wine after the guests have had too much to drink; but you have saved the best till now."
JOHN 2:1-10

I began to weep. The words I spoke the prior afternoon to my children came back to me: "All I do is pour the water." There was so much emotion surging through me as this Bible passage came alive and spoke to my innermost being. God began to soothe my frantic thoughts with His truth.

I do pour the water. And it's a privilege, not a burden. It's an act of obedience, because I'm called to do as He has told me. I pour love, truth, patience, and kindness. I pour wise instruction with advice, such as "It's better to give than to receive," "Apologize when you hurt someone," "Give charitable judgment," and "Don't conform to the pattern of the world." I pour service by managing our home through organizing, cleaning, and cooking. I pour memories and nurturing through laughter, nature walks, cuddle time, blowing bubbles, and book reading. All of it. I do all of it. Pour. Pour. Pour.

List some of the ways you pour into your children.

We pour again and again because Jesus told us to. As an act of obedience, we pour through service and sacrifice into our children, and He turns it into wine. Even if no one else knows how it got there or why—just as the master of the wedding banquet didn't realize where the best wine had come from—God is fully aware of your every act of service for your family and what He intends to accomplish through each one.

God sees. God knows. And that is enough motivation for you to keep on pouring.

As the truth that we're called to "pour" washes over you, describe what you're thinking and feeling in this moment.

TAKE ACTION

Let's briefly head back over to 2 Peter 1.

> ⁵For this very reason, make every effort to add to your faith goodness; and to goodness, knowledge; ⁶and to knowledge, self-control; and to self-control, perseverance; and to perseverance, godliness; ⁷and to godliness, mutual affection; and to mutual affection, love. ⁸For if you possess these qualities in increasing measure, they will keep you from being ineffective and unproductive in your knowledge of our Lord Jesus Christ. ⁹But whoever does not have them is nearsighted and blind, forgetting that they have been cleansed from their past sins. ¹⁰Therefore, my brothers and sisters, make every effort to confirm your calling and election. For if you do these things, you will never stumble, ¹¹and you will receive a rich welcome into the eternal kingdom of our Lord and Savior Jesus Christ.
> 2 PETER 1:5-11

Verses 5-7 give us a series of qualities we should add to our lives. List them below.

Verse 8 says we should "possess these qualities in
_____ _____" and that we should
do that because "they will keep you from _____
_____ and _____ in your
knowledge of our Lord Jesus Christ."

Of all the qualities listed, which do you possess in the greatest measure? How can you grow in one of the other qualities?

Verses 9-11 share that, as a believer in and follower of Christ, you can and should live out your faith, that you are indeed cleansed from your sin, and once you receive Christ you will never be taken from Him. You will be welcomed and live eternally with Christ.

How can these verses encourage and fulfill you in the midst of the struggles of motherhood?

DIG DEEPER

If you've never accepted Christ as your Savior, I hope and pray you're recognizing His love for you, His desire to adopt you as His own, and His eagerness to walk with you daily as you pour into your children and teach them His ways. A relationship with Christ is the beginning of satiating the longing for the garden that is, as determined in week 2, what our hearts long to feel.

That personal relationship with Jesus will then equip you to teach your children His ways and ensure their eternity as well. If you have a desire to accept Christ, go to *www.lifeway.com/salvation* to learn more. Or you can pray a simple prayer, such as this one, wherever you are.

Dear God, I know I am a sinner. I believe Jesus died to forgive me of my sins. I now accept Your offer of eternal life. Thank You for forgiving me of all my sin. Thank You for my new life. From this day forward, I will choose to follow You.

If you'd like to speak with someone about how to have new life in Christ, stop by your local church to have a conversation with a staff person. Or, if you need help connecting to a local church or want to speak to someone now, call toll free 888.537.8720.

If you already have a relationship with Christ, would you please spend time right now in prayer for the moms who will be reading this and who don't yet know Him. There's no greater act of love that you could do right now.

DAY 3
POURING

Join me again in John 2:1-10, as we study Jesus' first miracle. Let's see how this miracle can further speak to us in our mom lives. Read all 10 verses again.

> [1]On the third day a wedding took place at Cana in Galilee. Jesus' mother was there, [2]and Jesus and his disciples had also been invited to the wedding. [3]When the wine was gone, Jesus' mother said to him, "They have no more wine."
> [4]"Woman, why do you involve me?" Jesus replied. "My hour has not yet come."
> [5]His mother said to the servants, "Do whatever he tells you."
> [6]Nearby stood six stone water jars, the kind used by the Jews for ceremonial washing, each holding from twenty to thirty gallons.
> [7]Jesus said to the servants, "Fill the jars with water"; so they filled them to the brim.
> [8]Then he told them, "Now draw some out and take it to the master of the banquet."
> They did so, [9]and the master of the banquet tasted the water that had been turned into wine. He did not realize where it had come from, though the servants who had drawn the water knew. Then he called the bridegroom aside [10]and said, "Everyone brings out the choice wine first and then the cheaper wine after the guests have had too much to drink; but you have saved the best till now."
> **JOHN 2:1-10**

Jesus had just started His earthly ministry and had begun gathering disciples when they were invited to a wedding in Cana. In that culture, weddings were a week-long celebration and much of the town would have been invited; Jesus and His disciples were just a few guests among many. Mary, Jesus' mother, was also there. It was she who informed Him that the hosts had run out of wine.

At this point, Jesus had worked no miracles. Why do you think Mary went to Him to solve the problem?

Jesus first responded by pointing out to her that He didn't intend to get involved because His time had not yet come—meaning the time to reveal Himself as the Messiah (which would've required performing miracles). But, as it turned out, this would be the occasion of His first miracle after all.

Think of the guests at this wedding. Isn't it typical human behavior to enjoy good times and celebrations without giving much thought to Jesus' involvement in them? But as soon as a problem or need arises, the first thing we do is go to Him and ask Him to solve the problem for us.

Describe a time recently when a need caused you to ask God for help.

It's certainly not wrong to go to God for help, because at least we're recognizing that He is the first one to whom we should turn. But what we often overlook is that sometimes Jesus uses the problem itself to strengthen us and to help us hear His voice in the matter.

What's interesting to me is that Jesus often uses methods that require our direct participation. Read verse 5 again:

His mother said to the servants, "Do whatever he tells you."
JOHN 2:5

These were the words of Jesus' mother, who understood who He was and that He was to be trusted, no matter how difficult the problem or unusual the instructions He gave. Mary advised those who didn't know Jesus as intimately as she did to do whatever He said.

Write out Jesus' instructions to the servants, found in verse 7.

If Jesus were to look into your eyes and utter those same words to you, how much easier would it be to fully devote yourself to doing what He instructs you to do as a mom?

TAKE ACTION

The problem with pouring and filling is that we get so tired of it. How many times have we admitted—at least to ourselves—that we've grown weary of pouring? Left unchecked, that weariness easily brings discouragement, which often causes us to ignore what Jesus told us to do in the first place. So we quit pouring.

How would this have played out at the wedding in Cana? Think of the servants and what murmurings and grumblings might've been going on in their hearts. Their supervisor had told them to serve the guests wine, yet at the urging of one of the guests, they were being told to pour water—when wine was what was needed! Why should they waste time pouring water into jars, which by the way were so large and heavy they couldn't move them? The servants had to traipse back and forth, repeatedly doing the same monotonous, unexciting, uncelebrated, seemingly pointless work of pouring water into stone jars. Can you relate?

In the meantime, the wedding guests were feasting and probably had no idea what was going on. They didn't know what the servants were doing or Who told them to do it. Nor did they care unless their wine glasses were empty. The water pourers went unnoticed.

The task the servants were given was all the more confusing because they were told to pour the water into jars that the guests would've used to take a quick sponge bath! These were not where one would go for a refreshing drink of water. Monotony, obscurity, and a puzzling assignment were all part of the wedding servants' lives that day.

> *Perhaps those things are a part of your life today. Share ways in which you've felt your job as a mom has had monotonous or puzzling assignments that don't make sense for you to be doing.*

How many times in our weakened or tired conditions have we either questioned God or neglected to pour? I know I've thought, and said, *I deserve a break*. Surely the wine pourers had personal things they wanted to do, and may have been anxious to leave the wedding feast so they could get on with those plans. Why continue to serve others? If the wine ran out, shouldn't it have been time to clock out and have some "me" time? Mom, please make time for you, but make sure you keep pouring into your children. You never know when the next drop could be exactly what their little souls need.

DIG DEEPER

Yes, the things we do as mothers will often go unnoticed, just as the wine pourers were unnoticed. The laborious tasks of motherhood are rarely heralded, while endeavors we may seek outside of mothering are more likely to be rewarded with a paycheck, a certificate of appreciation, a pat on the back, or some sort of recognition for the effort.

Still, after reading John 2, we are in on a little secret about Jesus' first miracle.

What secret for moms do you think is found in Jesus' first miracle?

Jesus knew that the water the servants were carrying and pouring would soon become the finest wine any of the guests had ever tasted. Jesus knew what the outcome would be; the servants just needed to trust. And pour.

What is it God has asked you to do that makes no sense, but He is asking you to just "pour the water" and trust Him with the outcome?

The servants' obedience to Jesus is a picture of how we as mothers should go about doing what He has assigned to us. When Jesus asked them to fill the water jars and then instructed them to pour water into a wine glass and give it to the head steward, they had no idea why or how that made any sense. But they obeyed. They carried. They poured. They served.

Will you?

Pray, asking God to help you faithfully serve without knowing the outcome. Also pray for the future of your children, whose futures He holds.

DAY 4
KEEP POURING!

I'm beyond excited to continue to share with you what God has revealed to me through this first miracle, and I ask that you take just a moment to bow in prayer, asking Him to reveal truths specific to your circumstances through today's time in His Word.

The ordinary water that was painstakingly poured into those stone water jars gave no clues as to its ultimate importance. Workers, who had been laboring for days, were no doubt weary from the many acts of service they had been performing at the wedding feast. Each of those stone jars held approximately 20 gallons of water. What if, in their weariness, the servants had poured them only half full? It would have been a valiant attempt based on their circumstances. And who could fault them? That's still at least 60 gallons.

Many of us reach a point in our day, or in our lives, when we've grown weary or when other voices pull us away from what God has called us to do in our mom lives. We sometimes think if we don't do the daily, seemingly pointless mothering tasks that influence who our children become, what will the world really lose? So we leave the jars half empty, too tired to continue to pour.

Mom, when you're weary, stop and pray for God to give you the strength and wisdom you need for today. Allow His perfect grace and mercy to reinforce you at all times but certainly when your best just doesn't seem good enough.

> *Write out a prayer that God would give you the stamina to keep pouring and not grow weary.*

The problem is we're not really talking about stone jars and water, are we? We're talking about our children's lives. When it comes to our kids, the space not filled with Jesus' best will get filled with something else. And that something is at best a time-waster and at worst a soul-destroyer—from the wasteland of overindulgence in video games, movies, and all things digital to destructive relationships, drugs and alcohol, and immorality.

We must keep pouring.

TAKE ACTION

Sometimes our children reach an age, usually in the tween and teen years, when they try to convince us that it's no longer necessary for us to fill them; they've "got this" and they don't need us anymore. But I say that this is when the pouring is at its most important, because what ends up being poured into a half-filled jar can spoil the wine.

List some of the dangers lurking out there for our children—things seeking to devour them earlier and earlier in life.

Take time to consider how half-filled jars can result in good wine being spoiled. Ask God to reveal areas in your children's lives that could be in danger of being tainted.

Now list practical ways you can combat this potential spoilage.

What's the difference between continuing to pour into your children and allowing them the space to grow up and make some mistakes on their own?

DIG DEEPER

When the master of the banquet was given a taste of the celestial offering, he marveled that while the best wine was usually served at the beginning of the feast, on this occasion, it had been saved for later—a pleasant surprise and a blessing for the guests.

Filling our children is our legacy, and the full outcome lies in a future we cannot see. As parents who do the pouring, we work through time, care, and God's guidance to age them toward His perfection.

God has given you the privilege of being a mom, and in that role, you also pour yourself out for your family, ever mindful to look ahead toward the blessing of a strong legacy. Rather than focus on the daily frustrations and challenges, recognize that your life can be a shining example of God's goodness. After all, your ultimate purpose is to bring glory to Him.

> So that you may become blameless and pure, "children of God without fault in a warped and crooked generation." Then you will shine among them like stars in the sky as you hold firmly to the word of life. And then I will be able to boast on the day of Christ that I did not run or labor in vain. But even if I am being poured out like a drink offering on the sacrifice and service coming from your faith, I am glad and rejoice with all of you.
> **PHILIPPIANS 2:15-17**

What is God's responsibility and what is yours for achieving His purposes with your children?

Truly, a mother's attention and care to pour into the lives of her children is a joyful and recurring act of humbling herself in service to others. In doing so, she is a living testimony of Jesus and always serving His best.

What things can you do to remind yourself of the joy and blessing of raising children in the midst of daily challenges?

FOR MOMS OF INFANTS, WHEN YOU'RE TIRED OF POURING

If you're like me, perhaps at times your thoughts lead you down a path you aren't intended to go. In an overwhelming moment, your mind takes over, eliciting untruths your heart aches to embrace and your ears long to hear:

I feel so small. I feel completely forgotten.

I can't do this. It requires too much.

My longing for sleep is interrupted by the sound of crying. Again. It's as if my brain is melting. My past, my memories, my education, relationships, knowledge, goals, and dreams are all losing their intended usefulness, melding into a putrid mess.

I no longer exist.

I've become a "what could have been" cliché.

I don't matter anymore.

I'm losing my chance at success and life fulfillment.

Another shrill cry wafting from the nursery—louder this time.

Why me? Why must it be me that answers the cry? I don't want to do this anymore.
It requires far too much.

Like the walking dead, or a silent drone on a mission, I do what I must do to stop the cries.

Tiny hands clasp bare skin, and I hear gurgling as my eyes travel down. I stare blankly at the wriggling baby in my arms. Little, bright eyes grow wider and light up, which awakens my dulled heart—and I hear a whisper from above, "You are highly favored."

A slideshow on the blessings of my life begin to click through my clouded head. What I grasp in the recognition of much blessing is the knowledge motherhood is more than simple provision; it's God's unmerited grace. The zombie-induced bitterness that had taken hold of me shatters, and broken pieces are blown into oblivion as the Holy Spirit wafts in to breathe new life. My cheeks grow cold from the healing, salty tears streaming down.

I treasure up all these things and ponder them in my heart.

Lord, may I never see motherhood as a burden or interruption, but as the highly favored gift that it is. May my daily life as a mom bring glory to You. Guide me to willingly, joyfully give of myself fully and to gratefully receive your grace.

"All to Jesus I surrender ... All to Thee, my blessed Savior, I surrender all."[1]

GOD'S HEART FOR MOTHERHOOD

God has burdened me with a not-always-popular message to implore moms to honestly evaluate their priorities and motivations in their daily lives. Our children's futures are our priority during their growing up years. All decisions must be prayed over and personal sacrifices made for their best interests. What the world is offering us as women is secondary to what God has entrusted to us as moms. In the process of trusting God and His timing, He will pattern our steps and train us for His purposes.

God knows what that looks like for you, and He will guide you as you seek His will. Mom, congratulate yourself for already taking so many positive steps in your children's lives. No doubt you work hard and seek God's will for motherhood. Yet I pray that you will press on and continue to pray for God's guidance as you parent your children.

Motherhood is a noble, God-mandated role. Write how you believe that to be true in your own life.

Also, please pray for your friends who struggle in this way. Teach them what God teaches you. Through conversations and encouragement, help other moms who are carrying too much. Serve single moms. Encourage your church to serve single moms. Notice kids who are disconnected and influence them for God's purposes in their lives.

Who in your circle of influence needs encouragement? What children around you could use a positive mentor?

Read from Deuteronomy. Then underline or highlight what God asks of you regarding your children and the children He places in your path.

Hear, O Israel: The LORD our God, the LORD is one. Love the LORD your God with all your heart and with all your soul and with all your strength. These commandments that I give you today are to be on your hearts. Impress them on your children. Talk about them when you sit at home and when you walk along the road, when you lie down and when you get up.
DEUTERONOMY 6:4-7

What are your top priorities?

How are you seeking relationships with your children that lead to the ability to influence them?

How can you continually choose to pour, teaching your children as instructed by God?

Interestingly, Jesus did not call a lot of attention to Himself as He turned the water into wine—His first miracle no less! He was made aware of what needed to be done, chose to do it, and allowed the blessing to occur.

TAKE ACTION

Let's take the focus off ourselves and our children for a moment. My heart is breaking, and I'm weeping. We sometimes look for mission opportunities and miss the very mission opportunities in our homes, in our own neighborhoods, and in our communities.

The best way to serve joyfully in your own home is to find ways to serve outside of your home. After all, serving others is a great way for a thriving family to do life! It teaches a heart of gratitude and guards against entitlement. Your family doesn't have to go on a grand mission trip to another country to serve missionally; you can start by serving in your own community.

God has you and your family right where you are for a purpose. Be mindful to take notice of those in your neighborhood and those you come into contact with in your daily flow of life. God patterns your footsteps, so He knows whom He wants you to serve ... right where you are! So keep your head up and your eyes sharp, focusing on the needs around you. Begin a new emphasis on the importance of being a servant to those around you by getting the whole family involved!

Make a list of those who may need a helping hand and how your family can help. Better yet, here's the list; you just drop in the names.

☐ *Yard work for the elderly or infirmed*
☐ *A meal delivery to a single parent*
☐ *Respite childcare for adoptive or foster families*
☐ *Cookie/goodie bags to those who serve you*
☐ *A pizza and game night at your home with new friends*
☐ *An invitation to church and a Sunday meal*
☐ *Other:* _____

You can also serve, right in your home, by touching the lives of the kids God brings through your door. Through the years, I've had children who have shared with me how much they love being in our home, because we make time for them and pay attention to them. Never underestimate your power to positively influence children for God's purposes while they are in your home. Don't push the kids off into another room—join in the fun by playing games together, cooking together, doing projects together ... there's that word again—together!

Read Matthew 5:14-16. How does Jesus refer to those who share His love with others? What should your good deeds for others lead to?

DIG DEEPER

My heart leaps with joy as I picture your hands turning the pages in this Bible study. I marvel knowing that God purposed our time together here in these pages. God's ways are mysterious and amazing, and I hope He has revealed to you the wonder of the precious gift of motherhood.

Motherhood is indeed a high calling. We know this to be true because God chose it—just as He chose Mary to care for His own Son.

His own Son—whom God could've brought into this world through any means—had a mom. The Creator of all chose to have Jesus be born and nurtured by a mother. We must surmise from the obvious, hidden right in front of us, that motherhood—its constant care, intentional influence, and tenacious teaching—is vastly important to Father God.

Mary, the mother of Jesus went through a series of emotions upon learning that she was to be a mother. Read Luke 1:26-38 and write down the emotions the Scripture indicates, and those you might imagine she went through.

Take some time to ponder the humble beginnings of your foray into motherhood—whether it was well thought-out and planned, or whether, like Mary, you were given a surprise that wasn't in your plans.

Describe the details of the birth or "gotcha date" of one or all of your children.

Regardless of your plans, God had a plan.

> "For I know the plans I have for you," declares the LORD, "plans to prosper you and not to harm you, plans to give you hope and a future."
> **JEREMIAH 29:11**

Write this verse below, but replace the word "you" with your name.

Now let's go back to Mary's response.

> "I am the Lord's servant," Mary answered. "May your word to me be fulfilled." Then the angel left her.
> **LUKE 1:38**

Write that verse below.

Do you see it? After wrestling with what God was asking of her, Mary refers to herself as the Lord's *servant* and answers, "May it happen to me as you have said" (GNT)—a foreshadowing to Jesus' first miracle that has pierced our hearts this week as we contemplate serving from the perspective of Jesus' mom.

We've seen two verses for our mom hearts to hear, be challenged by, and encouraged with:

> "Do whatever He tells you" (John 2:5, HCSB).
> "May your word to me be fulfilled" (Luke 1:38).

You've been called by God to be a mom. I hope and pray that you will have the same open-hearted attitude as Mary to be a servant of the Lord as you pour yourself out. Whatever God has called your child to do, He has placed that child in your care for His purposes. Trust and obey.

Write a prayer to your Heavenly Father, graciously accepting that you are His servant and that your desire is for your life to be as He has said.

As our time draws to a close and we reflect on the last six weeks, I hope you embrace the truth that our Father, Provider, and Protector has built into the motherhood equation a felt need that causes us to seek Him and flee the tempting enemy—the exact opposite of what Eve laid before us as our destiny. Do you see the enormity of this? The demands of motherhood bring us to the end of ourselves and reveal a need in us that propels us straight to God, His love, and His truth. That is God's heart for motherhood.

Sweet Mom, I hope you've been encouraged to seek God in your everyday beautiful mess, and I pray you choose to be right where God wants you in the lives of your children. I pray you live every motherhood moment in His grip with expectant joy!

ENDNOTES

Week 2

1. Quote from *Moms' Night Out*. This saying originated from the poem, "The Hand That Rocks The Cradle Is The Hand That Rules The World" by William Ross Wallace (1865). The poem praises motherhood.

2. From the sermon "Who Is My Neighbor?" by Pastor Tim Lundy, Fellowship Bible Church, Little Rock, AR. 25 April 2010.

3. "*Philoteknos*" (Titus 2:4), Blue Letter Bible. Cited 14 March 2014. Available from the Internet: *www.blueletterbible.org*.

4. Phillip Yancey, *Reaching for the Invisible God* (Grand Rapids, MI: Zondervan, 2000), 84.

Week 6

1. "I Surrender All," Words by Judson W. Van DeVenter. Music by Winfield S. Weeden. *Baptist Hymnal* (Nashville, TN: LifeWay Worship, 2008), 433.

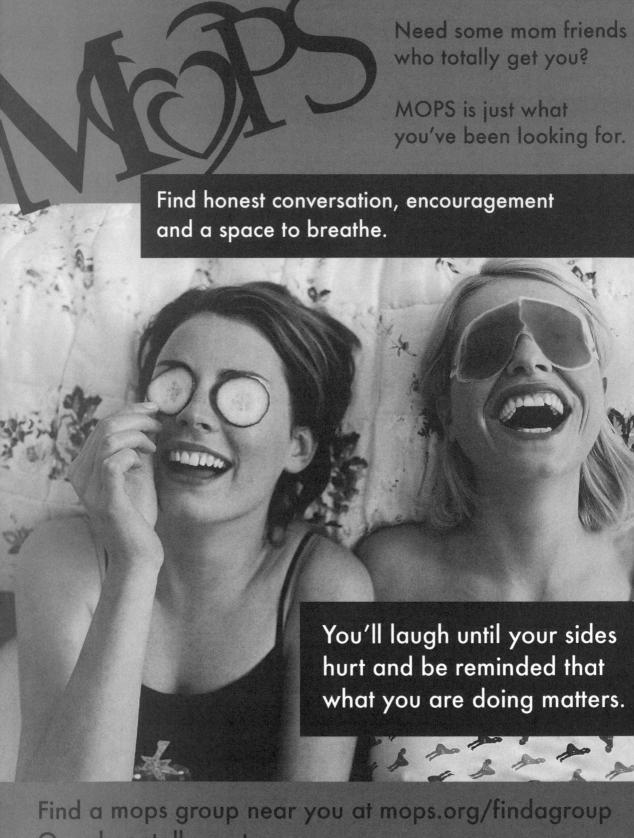

LET'S BE FRIENDS!